A Writing Process Book

interactions one

A Writing Process Book

Third Edition

interactions one

Margaret Keenan Segal

Cheryl Pavlik

With contributions by Laurie Blass

The McGraw-Hill Companies, Inc.

New York   St. Louis   San Francisco   Auckland   Bogotá   Caracas   Lisbon
London   Madrid   Mexico City   Milan   Montreal   New Delhi   San Juan
Singapore   Sydney   Tokyo   Toronto

This is an EDI book.

McGraw-Hill

A Division of The McGraw-Hill Companies

Interactions One
A Writing Process Book
Third Edition

1 2 3 4 5 6 7 8 9 0   DOC DOC   9 0 9 8 7 6

ISBN 0-07-055030-1
ISBN 0-07-114371-8

This book was set in Times Roman by Monotype Composition Company, Inc.

The editors were Tim Stookesberry, Bill Preston, and Eden Temko, the designers were Lorna
Lo, Suzanne Montazer, Francis Owens, and Elizabeth Williamson; the production supervisor
was Patricia Myers; the cover was designed by Francis Owens; the cover illustrator was Susan
Pizzo; the photo researcher was Cindy Robinson, Seaside Publishing; illustrations were done by
David Bohn, Axelle Fortier, Rick Hackney, Lori Heckelman, and Sally Richardson.

R. R. Donnelley & Sons Company, Crawfordsville, IN, was printer and binder.
Phoenix Color Corporation was cover separator and printer.

Library of Congress Catalog Card Number: 95-80475.

INTERNATIONAL EDITION

When ordering this title, use ISBN 0-07-114371-8.

Photo credits: *Page 1* © Frank Tapia; *13* © John Fung; *14* © Everett Collection; *31* © Merritt
Vincent / PhotoEdit; *33* © Tom McCarthy / PhotoEdit; *38 (top)* © Michael Newman /
PhotoEdit; *(bottom)* © K. Preuss / The Image Works; *43* © Beryl Goldberg; *47* © Jeff Green-
berg, MRP / Photo Researchers, Inc.; *48 (top left)* © Robert Brenner / PhotoEdit; *(top right)* ©
Vic Bider / PhotoEdit; *(bottom left)* © Jeff Greenberg, MRP / Photo Researchers, Inc.; *(bottom
right)* © Peter Menzel / Stock, Boston, *49* © Walter Gilardetti; *59* © Beryl Goldberg; *71* ©
Billy E. Barnes / PhotoEdit; *80* © Beryl Goldberg; *85* © Phil McCarten / PhotoEdit;

(continued on page 180)

Contents

Preface
to the Third Edition

The Interactions One Program

The Interactions One program consists of five texts and a variety of supplemental materials for high-beginning to low-intermediate students seeking to improve their English language skills. Each of the five texts in this program is carefully organized by chapter theme, vocabulary, grammar structures, and, where possible, language functions. As a result, information introduced in a chapter of any one of the Interactions One texts corresponds to and reinforces material taught in the same chapter of the other four books, creating a truly integrated, four-skills approach.

The Interactions One program is highly flexible. The texts in this series may be used together or separately, depending on students' needs and course goals. The books in this program include:

- **A Communicative Grammar.** Organized around grammatical topics, this book includes notional/functional material where appropriate. It presents all grammar in context and contains many types of communicative activities.
- **A Listening / Speaking Skills Book.** This book uses lively, natural language from various contexts, including dialogues, interviews, lectures, and announcements. Listening strategies emphasized include summarizing main ideas, making inferences, listening for stressed words, reductions, and intonation.
- **A Reading Skills Book.** The reading selections contain sophisticated college-level material; however, vocabulary and grammar have been carefully controlled to be at students' level of comprehension. The text includes many vocabulary-building exercises and emphasizes reading strategies such as

skimming, scanning, guessing meaning from context, understanding the structure and organization of a selection, increasing reading speed, and interpreting the author's point of view.
- **A Writing Process Book.** This book uses a process approach to writing, including many exercises on prewriting and revision. Exercises build skills in exploring and organizing ideas; developing vocabulary; using correct form and mechanics; using coherent structure; and editing, revising, and using feedback to create a final draft.
- **A Multi-Skills Activity Book.** New to this edition, this text gives integrated practice in all four language skills. Among the communicative activities included in this text are exercises for the new video program that accompanies the Interactions One series.

Supplemental Materials

In addition to the five core texts outlined above, various supplemental materials are available to assist users of the third edition, including:

Instructor's Manual/Test Bank

Extensively revised for the new edition, this manual provides instructions and guidelines for using the five core texts separately or in various combinations to suit particular program needs. For each of the core texts, there is a separate section with teaching tips, additional activities, and other suggestions. The testing materials have been greatly expanded in this edition.

Audio Program for Interactions One: A Listening/Speaking Skills Book

 Completely rerecorded for the new edition, the audio program is designed to be used in conjunction with those exercises that are indicated with a cassette icon in the student text. Complete tapescripts for all exercises are now included in the back of the student text.

Audio Program to Accompany Interactions One: A Reading Skills Book

 This new optional audio program contains selected readings from the student text. Readings that are included in this program are indicated with a cassette icon in the student text.

Video

New to this edition, the video program for Interactions One contains authentic television segments that are coordinated with the twelve chapter themes in the five texts. Exercises and activities for this video are in the Multi-Skills Activities Book.

Interactions One: A Writing Process Book, Third Edition

Interactions One: A Writing Process Book, third edition, was designed to lead students through the writing process and provide an assortment of activities to help them master the wide array of writing skills necessary for good writing.

Each of the twelve chapters in this text is divided into a number of distinct sections focusing on different steps in the writing process. These sections introduce various writing strate-gies and techniques and allow students to practice them one step at a time. This practice helps students understand how the different techniques work before they use them in their own writing. Students are given specific guidance in using their new skills to generate and organize ideas and to write, edit, and revise paragraphs of their own. At every step, students are encouraged to analyze and discuss the strategies they are using; in this way, students focus on one skill at a time. Beginning students especially benefit from this step-by-step approach because they are usually more comfortable with structured practice. By the end of each chapter, the students will have acquired new skills and produced their own paragraphs.

Special appendixes at the end of the book provide spelling, punctuation, and capitalization rules that students can use for reference. There are also feedback sheets for the instructor's use (see Teaching Suggestions, page ix).

Although the concept of writing as a process is central to the course, traditional areas of instruction such as paragraph form, mechanics, and grammar are practiced throughout. The emphasis, however, is on grammatical and lexical features that serve to unify a paragraph.

Our own classroom exerience shows that the analysis of model paragraphs can be helpful and instructive. Therefore, the chapters also contain two or three tasks based on model paragraphs.

Chapter Organization

1. **Exploring Ideas.** The first problem that most students encounter is a difficulty in generating ideas. This section teaches strategies to help them with that task. Some of the methods presented are discussing and listing ideas, interviewing, and free writing. A vocabulary-building activity gives students some of the language they may need in writing their own paragraphs and encourages them to use fellow students and their teachers as resources for additional vocabulary development.

2. **Organizing Ideas.** In this section, students are taught organizational skills such as writing effective topic sentences, limiting the information in a paragraph, and organizing different types of paragraphs.

3. **Developing Cohesion and Style.** This section focuses on the grammatical and lexical features that unity a paragraph. Students are taught the most natural use of structures and vocabulary in extended written discourse. Some sentence-level structures that often cause students problems, such as choice of tense, are also covered in this section.

4. **Writing the First Draft.** Because most students do not realize that good writing is usually the product of many revisions, they are explicitly told that the first paragraph they write is only a draft.

5. **Editing Practice.** One of the most important skills for students to master is the ability to edit their own work. This section gives them paragraphs that contain common errors of form, grammar, cohesion, and organization. By finding errors in compositions they have not written, students learn to critically evaluate their own work with less anxiety. A positive approach to this step is recommended. Do not expect students to find all errors; having students work in small groups can make this activity more fun.

6. **Editing Your Writing.** After students practice editing other paragraphs, they are asked to edit their own compositions. Teachers can ask students to focus on specific aspects of their writing to make this task less frustrating. We also suggest that students work with partners so they can help each other with this important step.

7. **Writing the Second Draft.** Only after students have had a chance to revise and edit their own compositions are they required to hand in neatly written papers for the teacher's evaluation.

A Step Beyond. Too often, students' interest in their writing ends once they receive a grade. This final section provides a variety of additional activities to encourage students to communicate with each other through their writing. Suggestions include using writing as the basis of debate or discussion, creating class books with student paragraphs, and displaying writing on bulletin boards. Unstructured journal writing assignments, both on and off the chapter topic, are also featured here for extra writing practice.

Teaching Suggestions

This book has been designed for four hours of classwork per chapter, with homework assignments after each class. Some groups may require more classroom time. Although the text provides a set format, it should not be considered prescriptive. More sophisticated students who may have already developed their own writing strategies should not be forced to abandon them. In addition, we recommend that you ask students to do as much extra free writing as possible; the *Instructor's Manual* contains additional suggestions for assigning unstructured writing work.

Many activities in the book are described as group work and are denoted as such by the group icon. Although teachers should feel free to adapt the tasks according to the needs and abilities of their own students, we feel that group and pair work help students develop self-confidence. Because writing is such a daunting task for most students, working with others may help them see that all students have many of the same difficulties.

The feedback sheets at the end of the book help teachers organize their comments in a way that students can easily interpret. Teachers are encouraged to give as much positive feedback as possible, to focus on content before grammar, and to concentrate on those skills that are presented in each particular chapter. This practice is especially vital for beginning students, whose mistakes are so numerous.

New to the Third Edition

The third edition of *Interactions One: A Writing Process Book* remains dedicated to providing students with a variety of activities that guide them through the process of writing. However, each chapter of the third edition includes many new features; here are the highlights.

1. **Streamlined Design.** The new edition features an attractive two-color design and an extensively revised art program. These changes were initiated to make the books more appealing, up-to-date, and user-friendly. In addition, we made the books easier to use by simplifying and/or eliminating complicated direction lines, numbering all exercises and activities, and highlighting key information in shaded boxes and charts.

2. **Revised Chapter Organization.** We streamlined the chapter organization in the third edition by collapsing some of the writing process steps, creating an easy-to-follow seven-step sequence (see Chapter Organization, page viii).

3. **New Chapter Theme on Science and Technology.** The third edition of the Interactions One program features an entirely new theme for Chapter Eleven: Science and Technology. The technology aspects of this new chapter theme are stressed in *A Writing Process Book* as students are exposed to the changing world of written communication in the age of the Internet, the great electronic "superhighway." In addition, the themes for several other chapters have been broadened to include new content.

4. **What Do You Think?** These new boxed features in each chapter encourage students to relate their personal experiences to an aspect of the chapter theme and to develop their critical thinking skills. Many of these new features include communicative group and/or pair activities, and some provide additional writing activities (including journal writing).

5. **Focus On Testing.** Chapters Seven through Twelve contain these new boxed features, which are designed to help students prepare to take timed writing tests, such as the standardized tests like the TOEFL.

Acknowledgments

Our thanks to the following reviewers whose comments, both favorable and critical, were of great value in the development of the third edition of the Interactions/Mosaic series:

Jean Al-Sibai, University of North Carolina; Janet Alexander, Waterbury College; Roberta Alexander, San Diego City College; Julie Alpert, Santa Barbara City College; Anita Cook, Tidewater Community College; Anne Deal Beavers, Heald Business College; Larry Berking, Monroe Community College; Deborah Busch, Delaware County Community College; Patricia A. Card, Chaminade University of Honolulu; Jose A. Carmona, Hudson County Community College; Kathleen Carroll, Fontbonne College; Conseula Chase, Loyola University; Lee Chen, California State University; Karen Cheng, University of Malaya; Gaye Childress, University of North Texas; Maria Conforti, University of Colorado; Earsie A. de Feliz, Arkansas State University; Elizabeth Devlin-Foltz, Montgomery County Adult Education; Colleen Dick, San Francisco Institute of English; Marta Dmytrenko-Ahrabian, Wayne State University; Margo Duffy, Northeast Wisconsin Technical; Magali Duignan, Augusta College; Janet Dyar, Meridian Community College; Anne Ediger, San Diego City College; D. Frangie, Wayne State University; Robert Geryk, Wayne State University; Jeanne Gibson, American Language Academy; Kathleen Walsh Greene, Rhode Island College; Myra Harada, San Diego Mesa College; Kristin Hathhorn, Eastern Washington University; Mary Herbert, University of California–Davis; Joyce Homick, Houston Community College; Catherine

Hutcheson, Texas Christian University; Suzie Johnston, Tyler Junior College; Donna Kauffman, Radford University; Emmie Lim, Cypress College; Patricia Mascarenas, Monte Vista Community School; Mark Mattison, Donnelly College; Diane Peak, Choate Rosemary Hall; James Pedersen, Irvine Valley College; Linda Quillan, Arkansas State University; Marnie Ramker, University of Illinois; Joan Roberts, The Doane Stuart School; Doralee Robertson, Jacksonville University; Ellen Rosen, Fullerton College; Jean Sawyer, American Language Academy; Frances Schulze, College of San Mateo; Sherrie R. Sellers, Brigham Young University; Tess M. Shafer, Edmonds Community College; Heinz F. Tengler, Lado International College; Sara Tipton, Wayne State University; Karen R. Vallejo, Brigham Young University; Susan Williams, University of Central Florida; Mary Shepard Wong, El Camino College; Cindy Yoder, Eastern Mennonite College; Cheryl L. Youtsey, Loyola University; Miriam Zahler, Wayne State University; Maria Zien, English Center, Miami; Yongmin Zhu, Los Medanos College; Norma Zorilla, Fresno Pacific College.

Summary of Writing Skills and Activities

Chapter	Rhetorical Focus	Organizing Skills	Grammar Focus
one	personal description	• interviewing • ordering information • writing topic sentences	• simple present tense • connecting ideas with *and, but, so,* and *also*
two	description (art)	• ordering information from general to specific	• present continuous tense • adding details using adjectives and prepositions • articles • pronouns
three	description (food)	• ordering information from general to specific • writing topic sentences	• count/noncount nouns • examples with *such as* • appositives
four	informal letter	• paragraphs in a letter	• modals *can, might, will* • imperatives • prepositions • *there* and *it* • the future: *be + going to*
five	autobiographical narration	• making a lifeline • limiting information • making paragraph notes • writing topic sentences	• simple past tense • combining sentences with time words and *because*
six	narration (mystery story)	• analyzing character • time sequence • limiting information • writing titles	• past continuous and simple past tenses • time clauses: *when , while, as* • *then* (transitional word) • *as soon as* • quotations

Editing Skills	Communicative Activities	Critical Thinking	Test Preparation Activities
• editing for content and form	• class newsletter • class paragraph • reading to improve writing	• fact vs. fiction	
• using articles	• describing a photo • writing a travel brochure	• comparing and contrasting	
• commas with appositives	• self-evaluation • sharing recipes • describing celebrations	• classifying and evaluating	
• the form of an informal letter	• replying to a letter • writing an invitation	• evaluating	
• punctuation with dependent clauses	• writing about a relative or friend	• generalizing	
• editing symbols	• writing a story with a partner • rewriting a story • writing an autobiographical story in the third person	• justifying opinions	

Summary of Writing Skills and Activities

Chapter	Rhetorical Focus	Organizing Skills	Grammar Focus
seven	exposition	• making an idea map • writing topic sentences	• restrictive relative clauses • transitional words and phrases: *in addition, for example, however* • showing purpose/giving reasons: *because* and infinitives
eight	summary (movie plot)	• categorizing • summarizing • writing a title	• historical present tense • adjectives • appositives
nine	biographical narration	• interviewing • writing topic sentences • writing concluding sentences	• present perfect and present perfect continuous tenses with *for* and *since* • using *in fact* • stating results with so. . . *that*
ten	classification (holidays)	• making an outline • ordering information according to importance	• *in addition to, besides, another* • ordinals: *first, second, third* • pronouns • quantifiers • nonrestrictive relative clauses
eleven	persuasion	• Internet etiquette • supporting opinions • writing newsgroup topic lines	• pronouns and synonyms • giving polite opinions and suggestions: *should, need to*
twelve	formal letter (complaint)	• identifying effective letters of complaint	• using past participles as adjectives • formal language in a business letter

Editing Skills	Communicative Activities	Critical Thinking	Test Preparation Activities
• more editing symbols	• class book of traditional treatments • describing an illness • comparing medical care in the United States and other countries	• comparing and contrasting	• recognizing correct usage of transitional phrases
• commas with adjectives and appositives	• evaluating movie summaries • evaluating movie reviews	• summarizing	• summarizing
• long forms in formal writing • spelling past and present participles	• class newsletter • guessing the subject of a biography • narration of past and future plans • group narration	• evaluating	• managing time for an essay test
• punctuating non-restrictive relative clauses	• class book on holidays • additional holiday topics	• examining meaning	• organizing ideas
• spelling and grammar in computer messages	• posting messages on computer or conventional bulletin boards • choosing newsgroup topics to write about	• expressing opinions	• making an outline of supporting examples and reasons
• following the format of a business letter	• replying to a letter of complaint • writing a letter of complaint about a school problem • reading newspaper complaint columns	• analyzing	• evaluating supporting details

CHAPTER **one**

School Life

in this chapter

You will interview a classmate and write an article about him or her for a class newsletter.

STEPS TO **writing**

1. Exploring Ideas
Interviewing Someone

A reporter for a school newspaper is writing an article about the new foreign students on campus. She is interviewing some of the students. Look at some of her questions.

1. What is your name?
2. Where are you from?
3. How do you usually spend your days here?
4. What do you like to do in your free time?
5. What is your occupation?
6. What do you like about the United States (or Canada)?

exercise 1

You are going to interview one of the students in your class for an article for a newsletter about your class. First write some questions. Use some of the questions above and write three other questions.

Your teacher will write some of your questions on the board. Discuss them. Are they good questions to ask? Now look at your questions. Are they good questions?

Choose the ten questions you like most. Then choose a partner and interview him or her. Write your partner's answers after the questions.

Building Vocabulary

How do you learn new vocabulary? One way to learn new words is to make vocabulary charts. For example, you can make a chart that lists new words by categories or topics. What new vocabulary did you and your partner use in your interview? Add your words to the following chart. Some words are there as examples.

WORK	FREE TIME ACTIVITIES	GOALS OR FIELDS	OTHER NEW VOCABULARY
waiter	swim	engineering	very much
		medical technology	

2. Organizing Ideas
Ordering Information in a Paragraph

There are different ways to organize or order information in a paragraph. For this kind of paragraph, write facts about the person you interview first. Then write the person's opinions.

 The reporter interviewed Yoshi Hiramoto for her article. After writing her notes, she numbered them in the order she wanted to write the sentences in her paragraph. Look at the reporter's questions and notes. Write F for questions about facts about Yoshi, O for questions about Yoshi's opinions, as in the example.

1. __F__   What is your name? <u>Yoshi Hiramoto</u>

2. _____   Where are you from? <u>Chiba – near Tokyo – seaport</u>

6. _____   How old are you? <u>34 years old</u>

7. _____   What is your occupation? <u>sales manager</u>

3. _____   Why are you in the United States? <u>needs English for job</u>

4. _____   What do you like about the United States? <u>likes class, likes Americans</u>

5. _____   What do you dislike about the United States? <u>doesn't like cafeteria food</u>

8. _____   How do you like this school? <u>very much, good English class</u>

9. _____   What do you like to do in your free time? <u>visits sights, rides bicycle</u>

 Write F or O in front of your questions and notes. Then number your questions in the order you want to write the sentences in your paragraph.

 Show your organization to the person you interviewed. Does she or he agree with it? Does she or he want to add any information?

Writing Topic Sentences

> The topic sentence tells the main idea of the paragraph. In your paragraph about the person you interviewed, the purpose of the topic sentence is to introduce your partner and tell something important about him or her. Don't begin paragraphs with "I am going to write about . . ." or "This paragraph is about . . ." Begin your paragraph with "(Name of student) is a member of (name of class) at (name of school)."

exercise 4   Write your topic sentence below.

_____

_____

3. Developing Cohesion and Style

Connecting Ideas

> Good writers connect the ideas in their paragraphs. A paragraph with connected ideas has cohesion. Good writers also use clear and simple language. This makes their writing easy to read. A paragraph with clear and simple English has good style.

 **exercise 1**   Look at the reporter's article and circle the words *and, but, so,* and *also.*

International Student at Eastern Community College

Yoshi Hiramoto is one of 350 International students at Eastern Community College. He is from Chiba, a seaport near Tokyo. Mr. Hiramoto is 34 years old and is a sales manager for a hospital equipment company. His company sells equipment to American hospitals, so he needs English for his work. Mr. Hiramoto likes the United States very much. He also likes the students at his school. He thinks his English class is excellent, but he thinks the food in the cafeteria is terrible. In his free time Mr. Hiramoto likes to bicycle and visit tourist sights near the school.

Using *and* to Connect Phrases

> When you want to say two things about a subject, use the word *and* to connect the verb phrases.
>
> *examples:*   Mr. Hiramoto is 34 years old *and* is a sales manager for a hospital equipment company.
>
> Brenda works during the day *and* goes to school at night.

 **exercise 2** Write sentences from the following phrases. Connect the phrases with *and*. The first one is done as an example.

Ming Su   is 26 years old
             is from Taiwan

Ming Su is 26 years old and is from Taiwan.

1. Amelia swims
            plays tennis

_____

_____

2. Reiko   is 19 years old
          likes music a lot

_____

_____

3. Salma   is married
          has two children

_____

_____

4. Enrique likes soccer
            plays every Saturday

_____

_____

Using *also* to Add Information

When two sentences give similar ideas, you can use the word *also* in the second sentence. Find the *also* in the reporter's paragraph about Yoshi Hiramoto. *Also* usually goes before the main verb in the sentence, but it goes after the verb *be*.

examples: Mr. Hiramoto likes the United States very much.
               He *also likes* the students in his school.
               Janet is in my English class.
               She *is /also* in a music class.

Use the caret symbol (ʌ) in corrections to add something to a sentence.

example: She is very pretty. She is ^also very intelligent.

 **exercise 3**   Use a ∧ to add *also* to these sentences.

1. He likes baseball. He likes rock music.

2. Hamid is tall. He is very athletic.

3. In her free time, Maddie plays basketball. She likes to swim.

4. Efraim works part-time. He takes care of his four children.

 **exercise 4**   Look at your notes from the interview. Write sentences that connect similar information with *and* and *also*. Show your sentences to your partner. Are the sentences correct?

Using *and, but,* and *so* to Connect Sentences

> You can connect two sentences with *and, but,* or *so.* Use a comma before these words when they connect two complete sentences.
>
> • *And* introduces additional information.
>
>   *example:*   Some schools offer everything from Asian studies to zoology. +
>   They have many recreational facilities and student services. =
>   Some schools offer everything from Asian studies to zoology, *and* they have many recreational facilities and student services.
>
> • *But* introduces contrasting information.
>
>   *example:*   He thinks his English class is excellent. +
>   He thinks the food in the cafeteria is terrible. =
>   He thinks his English class is excellent, *but* he thinks the food in the cafeteria is terrible.
>
> • *So* introduces a result.
>
>   *example:*   His company sells equipment to American hospitals. +
>   He needs English for his work. =
>   His company sells equipment to American hospitals, *so* he needs English for his work.

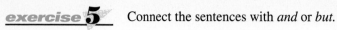

exercise 5   Connect the sentences with *and* or *but*.

1. Alberto lives with his sister. She drives him to school every afternoon.

   _____

   _____

2. Maria can speak English well. She needs more writing practice.

   _____

   _____

3. Western Adult School is in a beautiful location. It doesn't have very good library facilities.

   _____

   _____

4. The school offers a good program in business. Its recreational facilities are excellent.

   _____

   _____

exercise 6   Connect the sentences with *so* or *but*.

1. She has to work all day. She doesn't have time to do all her homework.

   _____

   _____

2. He likes his English class. He doesn't think the American students are very friendly.

   _____

   _____

3. Her company is opening an office in the United States. It needs English-speaking workers.

   _____

   _____

4. She likes school life. She is homesick for her family.

   _____

   _____

exercise 7   Look at your notes from the interview and write two or three sentences using *and,* *but,* and *so* to connect ideas.

_____

_____

_____

_____

_____

_____

_____

4. Writing the First Draft

When you write something important, you should write it at least two times. The first time you write is called the *first draft*. Write this draft quickly. Think about your ideas. Don't worry too much about grammar or form.

Write a paragraph about the person you interviewed. Use your organization and topic sentence from Exercises 3 and 4, page 4. You can also use some of your sentences with *and, so, but,* and *also.* Don't worry about writing everything correctly in this first draft. You can check it and rewrite it later.

5. Editing Practice
Editing for Content and Form

You should edit paragraphs at least two times.

- The first time you edit, focus on the content of the writing: the writer's ideas, and how they are organized and connected.
- The second time, focus on the form of the writing: the way the writing looks on the page, and the writer's grammar, spelling, and punctuation.

exercise 1 Edit the following paragraph for content. Focus only on the writer's ideas and organization. Think about the questions below. Make any corrections you think are necessary.

    1. Does the paragraph have a good topic sentence?
    2. Are all the sentences about one subject?
    3. Is the order of sentences correct?
    4. Can any sentences be connected?

A new class member

This is about Ana Maria vargas. is a new member of the English composition class at columbia Community College. There many classes at columbia. she generally likes her life in the United States, but she doesn't like her apartment. She is 28 years old. Ana Maria is from Peru. She is married she has three beautiful childs. her childs are young. so she no work right now. In her free time Ana maria sing and write songs.

exercise 2 Now edit the paragraph a second time. This time, focus on the form. Check the writer's use of third-person singular verbs in the present tense; they should end with -*s*. Check the writer's use of negative verb forms. Finally, check the writer's sentence and paragraph form. Use the following rules to help you. Make any corrections you think are necessary.

Rules for Sentence and Paragraph Form

  1. Write the title in the center of the first line.
  2. Capitalize all important words in the title.
  3. Don't capitalize small words like *a, the, to, with,* and *at* in titles, except at the beginning of a title.
  4. Skip a line between the title and the paragraph.
  5. Indent (leave a space) at the beginning of every paragraph.
  6. Begin every line except the first at the left margin. (Sometimes a line for the left margin is on the paper. If it isn't, leave a space of one inch.)
  7. Leave a one-inch margin on the right.
  8. Use a period (.) at the end of every sentence. (For rules on punctuation, see Appendix Three, pages 177 to 180, at the end of this book.)
  9. Leave a small space after the period.
10. Begin every sentence with a capital letter. (For rules on capitalization, see Appendix Two, pages 175 to 177.)

11. Also capitalize names of people and places. (See Appendix Two.)
12. If the last word of a line doesn't fit, use a hyphen (-) to break it. You can break a word only between syllables (**e•quip•ment**).
13. Periods and commas (,) must follow words. They can't begin a new line.
14. Every sentence in the paragraph follows the sentence before it. Start on a new line only when you begin a new paragraph.
15. In formal writing, most paragraphs have four to ten sentences. A paragraph usually has more than one or two sentences.

6. Editing Your Writing

Edit your first draft using the following checklist. First, edit your article for content, organization, and cohesion and style using items 1, 2, and 3 from the checklist. Then, edit it for grammar and form using items 4 and 5.

Editing Checklist

1. Content
   a. Is the information about your partner interesting?
   b. Is it complete?
   c. Is it correct?
2. Organization
   a. Are all the sentences about one topic?
   b. Is the order of the sentences easy to follow?
3. Cohesion and Style
   a. Are your sentences clear and simple?
   b. Are they easy to understand?
   c. Can you connect any sentences?
4. Grammar
   a. Is the grammar correct?
   b. Are your verbs correct? Remember that third-person singular verbs end with -*s* in the present tense. Also check that your negative verb forms are correct.
   c. Are singular and plural nouns correct?
   d. Is the word order in your sentence correct?
5. Form
   a. Is your punctuation correct?
   b. Is your spelling correct?
   c. Are your paragraph and sentence forms correct?

exercise 2 Show your article to the person you interviewed. Does she or he think the information in it is correct? Does she want to add anything to the paragraph? Does he think you should correct any of the grammar, spelling, punctuation, or sentence or paragraph form?

7. Writing the Second Draft

Rewrite your article using neat handwriting and correct form. Check the grammar and form one final time. Then give your article to your teacher for comments and corrections. When your teacher returns your paper, ask him or her about any comments or corrections you don't understand. The next time you write, look back at your teacher's comments. Follow your teacher's instructions, and try not to make the same mistakes again.

A STEP **beyond**

activity 1 Share your articles with your classmates. Read them aloud or pass them around the room.

activity 2 Your class can also make a class newsletter with your paragraphs. You can type or write neat copies of the corrected paragraphs. Give the newsletter a title and share it with other English classes.

As a class, interview your teacher. Write possible questions on the board. You can ask her or him:

1. Where are you from?
2. What do you like to do in your free time?
3. What do you like about your job?

Think of other questions too. Then write the paragraph together on the board. Different students can suggest different sentences. After you write all the sentences, edit the paragraph.

Do you know that reading automatically improves your writing? It is not important what you read—anything you enjoy reading will help you. Here are some things beginning students of English can read.

1. Special books written for beginning students of English as a Second Language have easy English but adult topics. Ask your teacher if your school has any of these special ESL readers you can borrow.
2. Books with pictures are easy to read. If you don't understand all the words, the pictures help. Comic books and children's books are excellent "picture books" for beginning students.
3. Supermarket newspapers (called *tabloids*) are fun and easy to read—just don't believe everything you find in them. They often have stories— sometimes true, sometimes not—about crazy happenings and famous people in movies, TV, and sports.

Read for at least a half hour every day and see how your English improves.

Fact or Fiction?

Joan Chen, actress

Imagine that your favorite TV, movie, or sports star (or other famous person) is experiencing a change in his or her life. Maybe she is making a new movie or starting a new TV season. Try to read something about the star (in English or your native language) in a tabloid or popular magazine. Do you think what you read is true? Why or why not?

Then write an article such as you might find in a tabloid about the star's new life. (Remember, it doesn't have to be true!) Where is he or she? How does he or she spend his days? What does he or she like or dislike about his or her life and work? How about his or her love life? In small groups, exchange articles with your classmates. Do they think what you wrote is fact or fiction? Why?

Journal Writing

You are going to keep a journal in this class. Journals are free writing exercises: You write quickly about what you are thinking or feeling. This is for practice, so what you are saying is more important than grammar and form. Each time you write something, what you write is called an *entry*. You can buy a special notebook for your journal, or you can write entries on separate pieces of paper and keep them in a folder. Sometimes you will have a time limit, sometimes you won't.

For your first journal entry, choose one of the following topics.

1. Write for ten minutes about yourself. Write about how you are feeling, what you are doing, or what you think of your school or your English class. If you want, you can show your entry to your teacher or a classmate.

2. Sometimes people can remind us of animals. For example, a person may be strong and make us think of an elephant or a lion. Think of someone you know. What kind of animal is he or she like? Write about why she or he is like that animal.

3. Write about school life in your home country.

CHAPTER **two**

Experiencing Nature

Watson and the Shark. John Singleton Copley, U.S., 1738–1815. Oil on canvas; 72 × 90¹/₄ in (182.9 × 229.2 cm). Gift of Mrs. George von Lengerke Meyer. Courtesy, Museum of Fine Arts, Boston. © 1995, Museum of Fine Arts, Boston

in this chapter

You will describe the painting *Watson and the Shark* by John Singleton Copley.

1. Exploring Ideas

Describing a Scene

In small groups, discuss these questions about the picture on page 15.

1. What is the title of the painting?
2. What is a shark?
3. Which man is Watson? Why do you think he is naked?
4. How many people are in the picture?
5. What is happening in the picture?
6. How does the picture make you feel?
7. What can you see in the background? Where do you think this is happening? Why?
8. Do you think this really happened? Why or why not?
9. When do you think this scene happened?
10. Is the man going to die?

What do you know about sharks? Discuss what you know in small groups. Are there many sharks where you come from? Are they dangerous? What do you know about shark attacks? How many people do you think sharks kill every year?

Then look at page 18 to find out more about this painting and sharks.

Building Vocabulary

You are going to write a paragraph describing *Watson and the Shark*. To begin, think about the vocabulary you will need to write your paragraph. The chart below lists some words by parts of speech. These words are only examples. What new vocabulary did your group use in answering the questions in Exercise 1? Add your words to the chart. Find out the meaning of any words that you don't understand.

NOUNS	ADJECTIVES	VERBS	OTHER
rowboat	huge	reach	_____
shark	frightening	kill	_____
spear	dark	hold	_____
rope	afraid	try	_____

NOUNS	ADJECTIVES	VERBS	OTHER
oar	dramatic	attack	_____
background	naked	rescue	_____
ship	_____	_____	_____
teeth	_____	_____	_____
harbor	_____	_____	_____
_____	_____	_____	_____
_____	_____	_____	_____
_____	_____	_____	_____

In small groups, discuss the painting. Look at the different parts of the painting. What is going on? What are the different people doing? Use some of the new vocabulary from the chart and other words of your own. Add any other new words from your discussion to the chart.

2. Organizing Ideas
Ordering Information in a Paragraph

Descriptions often begin with general information—information that describes the whole picture. Then a writer writes specific information—information that describes smaller parts of the picture.

The first sentence in a paragraph is often the topic sentence. In a paragraph about a work of art, it tells the name of the painting and the name of the artist. (Notice that we underline or *italicize* names of works of art.)

Read the following paragraph, which describes the painting on page 18. Which sentences give general information? Which sentences give specific information?

This is a picture of a park on a warm and sunny day. It seems very peaceful. In the park there are many large trees. On the left you can see a lake with some small sailboats. There are people in the park. They might be European. Some people are walking, and some are lying or sitting on the grass. They are wearing old-fashioned clothes. The women are wearing long dresses, and some of them are carrying umbrellas. In the middle of the painting there is a small child. She is walking with her mother. I don't like this painting very much because the people seem bored.

George Seurat, French, 1859–1891, *A Sunday on La Grande Jatte–1848*; oil on canvas, 1884–1886, 207.5 × 308 cm, Helen Birch Bartlett Memorial Collection, 1926.224. Photograph © 1994, The Art Institute of Chicago. All Rights Reserved

 Underline the topic sentence in the paragraph.

 Find the sentence that tells you what the writer thinks about the painting. Draw two lines under it.

More about *Watson and the Shark*

The scene in *Watson and the Shark* really happened. Mr. Brook Watson was swimming in the Havana harbor in Cuba when the shark attacked. The shark bit his leg, but Mr. Watson did not die. He was a politician, and he wanted to get publicity, so he asked the American painter John Singleton Copley (1738–1815) to paint the scene. Watson later became Lord Mayor of London.

More about Sharks

No one knows for sure where the English word "shark" comes from. Some people think it is from the Mayan Indian word *xoc*, meaning shark. Others think it is from the German *schurke*, meaning a bad person. One meaning of the English word shark is a dishonest or clever person.

People all over the world are afraid of sharks. But sharks really are not very dangerous—they only kill about 25 people every year.

exercise 4   Here are a student's notes about the mural (wall painting) that follows, *The Conquest of Mexico*, by Diego Rivera. Number the sentences from 1 (most general) to 7 (most specific). Put the writer's opinion last. Show your organization to another student. Does she or he agree with it? More than one correct answer is possible.

a. _____ A man is looking at a gold necklace.

b. _____ Spanish soldiers are shooting guns and a cannon.

c. _____ The picture shows the cruelty of the conquest.

d. _____ Indians lie dead in the lower left corner.

e. _____ *The mural shows Spanish soldiers taking control of Mexico.*

f. _____ A priest holds a cross.

g. _____ Indian workers dig in the mines.

h. _____ A soldier with a knife stands over a dead Indian.

i. _____ An Indian with a bow and arrow kneels behind the Spanish soldiers.

Diego Rivera, *The Conquest of Mexico: Invaders Attack with Cannon and Firearms,* West Wall, 1929–1930. National Palace, Mexico City, Mexico. Schalkwijk - Art Resource, NY.

exercise 5   Now look again at *Watson and the Shark*. Which of the following sentences is a good topic sentence for a paragraph about the painting?

1. *Watson and the Shark* is a good painting.

2. In this painting there are some men in a boat.

3. The men in this painting are afraid.

4. *Watson and the Shark*, by John Singleton Copley, shows a dramatic rescue.

exercise 6   Write a sentence giving general information about *Watson and the Shark*.

 **exercise 7** Write some sentences giving more information about *Watson and the Shark*. Then number your sentences in order from general to specific.

exercise 8 Write a sentence giving your opinion of the painting.

3. Developing Cohesion and Style

Adding Details: Adjectives

Adjectives make descriptions more interesting. They can be in two different positions:

1. After the verbs *be, seem,* and *look.*

   examples: The men are *young.*
               The men look *horrified.*

   Note: If you want to use more than one adjective you can connect them with *and:* The shark is huge *and* frightening.

2. Before a noun.

   example: The *young* men are in a boat.

 **exercise 1** Look at the picture *Watson and the Shark* again. With a partner, make a list of adjectives to describe the following.

- the boat
- the weather
- the man in the water

- the clothes the men are wearing
- the shark
- the water

 **exercise 2** Add the adjectives from your list to the following sentences.

1. The boat is in the water. _____

_____

2. There is a shark in the water. _____

_____

3. The men are wearing clothes. _____

_____

4. The man in the water seems _____

_____

5. The weather looks _____ and _____

_____

Adding Details: Prepositional Phrases

Notice that the prepositional phrases can be at the beginning of a sentence or at the end.

examples: *In the park* there are many large trees.
              There are people *in the park.*

It is good to put prepositional phrases in different places—not always at the beginning of a sentence, for instance. That way the style of your writing will be more interesting.

 **exercise 3**   Look at the paragraph about the Seurat painting again. Underline all the phrases that show position (location of someone or something). Most phrases that show position begin with prepositions.

exercise 4   The following sentences describe the metalwork shown below, *The Tree of Life*, by the Haitian artist Georges Liautaud. Add one of the prepositional phrases from the following list to each sentence.

- at a table
- to the right
- out of the tree
- to the left
- under the tree of life
- in the center

1. _____ is the tree of life.

2. Two children are standing _____ .

3. A bird is flying _____ .

4. On the right are two people sitting _____ .

5. _____ a man and a woman and baby are in a boat.

6. _____ is a smaller tree.

The Tree of Life by George Liautaud. Sculpture from the collection of Seldon Rodman. Photo by Seldon Rodman.

 Look at the sentences you wrote about the painting *Watson and the Shark*. Rewrite them using prepositional phrases.

Using Pronouns

You can use pronouns to replace some nouns when you write a paragraph. Pronouns add variety to your writing and help to connect your ideas. Here are some examples of two kinds of pronouns.

	Singular	Plural	examples	notes
Subject Pronouns	I you he, she, it	we you they	**Seurat** was a French painter. **He** is famous today.	**He** and **him** both refer to **Seurat**.
Object Pronouns	me you him, her, it	us you them	I studied **him** in art history.	

 Circle all the pronouns in the paragraph about Seurat's painting of the park. Then draw arrows to connect the pronouns to the nouns they represent.

 Read the following paragraph about the painting *The Boating Party* on page 23. Change some of the nouns to pronouns. Then compare your new paragraph with a classmate's. Are the changes the same in both paragraphs?

The painting *The Boating Party* is by Mary Cassatt. Three people are riding in a boat on the water. The painting shows only part of the boat. A woman and a child are sitting in the front of the boat. The woman is holding the child on her lap. A man is sitting in the middle of the boat. The man is rowing the boat and is facing the woman and child. The man is wearing black clothes. The woman and child are watching the man row. It is a beautiful day, and the man, woman, and child are having a good time.

Mary Cassatt. *The Boating Party*, Chester Dale Collection, © 1995 Board of Trustees, National Gallery of Art, Washington, 1893–1894, oil on canvas. 0. 900 × 1.173 (35$^7/_{16}$ × 46$^1/_8$); framed 1.21 × 1.378 (44$^1/_8$ × 54$^1/_4$).

Using Present Continuous

You can use the present continuous form of a verb to tell what is happening in a picture. Present continuous verbs have two parts:

the verb *be* (*is, are*)   +   verb + *ing*

examples: Watson *is swimming* near the shark.
        The men *are trying* to help Watson.

   In the paragraph about *The Boating Party* on page 22, underline the present continuous forms of the verbs. You should find nine examples.

 **exercise 10** Write the present participles of the following verbs. Use the spelling rules below to help you. The first one is done as an example.

1. swim _____swimming_____   6. attack _____

2. rescue _____   7. look _____

3. try _____   8. bite _____

4. throw _____   9. see _____

5. stand _____   10. refer _____

Spelling Rules for Adding *-ing* to a Verb

1. If the simple form of the verb ends in a silent *-e* after a consonant, drop the *-e* and add *-ing*.

   examples: race/racing   move/moving

2. If the simple form ends in *-ie*, change the *-ie* to *y* and add *-ing*.

   examples: die/dying   untie/untying

3. If the simple form is one syllable and ends in one consonant after one vowel, double the last consonant (except *x*) and add *-ing*.

   examples: run/running   get/getting

   Note that *w* and *y* at the end of words are vowels, not consonants.

4. If the simple form ends in a stressed syllable, follow the rule above for one final consonant after one vowel.

   example: begin/beginning

   If the last syllable is not stressed, just add *-ing*.

   example: happen/happening

5. In all other cases, add *-ing* to the simple form.

---

4. Writing the First Draft

Write a paragraph about the painting *Watson and the Shark*. Use your notes. Remember to use the present continuous to tell what's happening. Use *there is* and *there are* to name the things in the painting. Don't worry about mistakes. You can correct them later.

5. Editing Practice

Using Articles: *a/an* and *the*

A, *an*, and *the* are articles. They appear before nouns. *A* and *an* are indefinite articles. They describe general nouns. *The* is a definite article. It describes specific nouns.

	examples	notes
Indefinite Articles	A: I can drive a car, but I can't fly *an* airplane. B: Really? I can do both.	The speakers are talking about cars and airplanes in general—*any* cars or airplanes.
Definite Articles	C: Are you finished writing *the* reports yet? D: Not yet. Do you want to use *the* computer? C: That's all right. I can wait.	The speakers are talking about specific reports and a specific computer—the reports *that D is writing* and the computer *that D is using*.

Usually *a* or *an* comes before a noun when the noun appears for the first time. After that, *the* appears before the noun.

examples	notes
This is *a* painting of *an* island near Paris. *The* painting is very famous.	It is *one* painting of *one* island. It is *the* specific painting described in the first sentence.

exercise 1   Complete this paragraph about *The Tree of Life* with *a*, *an*, or *the*.

_____ large tree is in the middle. Two children are standing under _____ tree,

     1   2
and two children are climbing in _____ tree. _____ children are waving. On

                                    3   4
the left is _____ man and _____ woman in _____ boat. _____ man is fishing.

              5   6   7   8
_____ woman is holding _____ child. _____ large bird is flying over _____ boat.

   9   10   11   12
To the right is _____ smaller tree. Two people are sitting under _____ tree

               13   14
at _____ table. On _____ table is _____ plant.

   15   16   17

Edit the following paragraph twice and rewrite it correctly. The first time, check the organization of the paragraph. Does it move from general to specific? Do you need to change the order of the sentences? The second time, check it for correct use of *a/an* and *the*. Make any other changes you think are necessary. (*Hint:* There are five incorrect uses of *a/an* and *the*.)

The Starry Night is the painting by Vincent van Gogh, an Dutch artist. There are some other houses and buildings around a church. In the front of the painting are some tall, curving trees, and in the back are some rolling mountains. Our eyes follow their shapes up, around, down, and back again, like a ride on a roller coaster. In the center is a church. The stars, trees, and mountains look like they are moving. I like a painting because it reminds me of the making of the universe. It is the beautiful scene of a sky full of bright stars.

Vincent van Gogh. *The Starry Night* (1889). Oil on canvas, 29 × 36 $\frac{1}{4}$". The Museum of Modern Art, New York. Acquired through the Lillie P. Bliss Bequest. Photograph © 1995 The Museum of Modern Art, New York.

Interactions I • Writing

6. Editing Your Writing

 Edit your paragraph using the following checklist.

Editing Checklist

1. Content
   a. Are there interesting adjectives in the paragraph?
   b. Do the adjectives describe the picture well?
2. Organization
   a. Does the paragraph move from general to specific?
   b. Do you need to change the order of the sentences?
3. Cohesion and Style
   a. Can you connect any sentences?
   b. Are the pronouns correct?
   c. Are the adjectives in the correct place?
   d. Are the prepositional phrases appropriate?
4. Grammar
   a. Are the verb forms correct? Is there an *-s* on all third-person singular verbs?
   b. Is the use of *a/an* and *the* correct?
   c. Are the present participles correct?
5. Form
   Does the paragraph follow the rules for correct form? If you aren't sure, look back at the rules for sentence and paragraph form on pages 10 and 11.

 Show your paragraph to another student. He or she will check your work and tell you if anything in unclear.

7. Writing the Second Draft

Write the second draft of your description using neat handwriting and correct form. Check the form and grammar one more time. Then give it to your teacher for comments and corrections. When your teacher returns your paragraph, compare it with your paragraph from Chapter One. Do you see any improvements? What problems do you still have?

WHAT DO YOU THINK?

Comparing and Contrasting Art

Diego Rivera. *Rain (La lluvia)*. Mural, 2.05 x 2.284 m. Cou[rt]
of Fiestas, level 3, West Wall. Painted ca. July 1923–early
1924, Secretaria de Education Publica, Mexico City, Mexi[co].
Schalkwijk - Art Resource, NY.

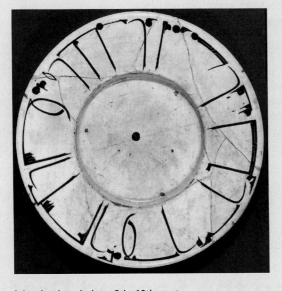

Islamic glazed plate, 9th–10th century

1. **Look at the different kinds of art above and discuss them in small groups. First describe each work of art. Can other students tell you more about the kinds of art you see? Can you see any of these kinds of art in your country?**
2. **Write a few sentences comparing the different kinds of art. Answer these questions. The first one is an example.**
   a. **What do the Rivera mural and the African art both show?**
   The Rivera mural and the African art both show people doing things.

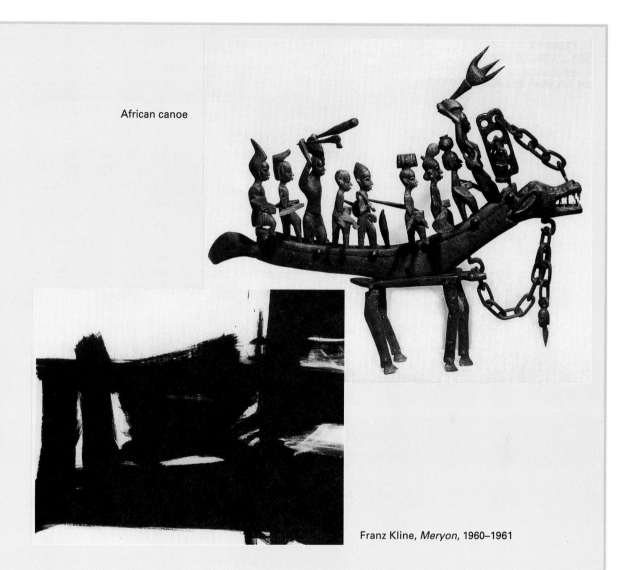

African canoe

Franz Kline, *Meryon*, 1960–1961

b. **What can you see in both the Islamic art and the Rivera mural?**
c. **What don't you see in the Islamic plate or the Kline painting?**
d. **How is the Kline painting different from the Rivera mural?**
e. **Which art is old? Which is new?**
f. **Which art do you like? Why?**
g. **Which art don't you like? Why not?**

A STEP beyond

 Find a picture or a photo of a scene from your home country, or describe a scene that you remember. First, write about the picture. What can you see in it? Are there any people there? What are they doing? Then edit your description. Have another student help you.

 Your teacher will collect your pictures from Activity 1 and put them in the front of the room so no one knows which picture belongs to which student. Then you and your classmates will read your descriptions to the class. Guess which picture each student is describing or which description doesn't have a picture.

 Pretend you are writing a travel brochure about your home country. Describe the country. Why should tourists visit there? What will they like? What interesting, beautiful, or historical sights are there to see? Bring in pictures if you can and make a travel brochure with your pictures and descriptions.

Journal Writing

 Choose one of the following topics.

1. Look at the different kinds of art on pages 28 and 29 again. Both the Islamic dish and the mural *Rain* contain writing. The writing on the dish says:

   > The beginning of knowledge is bitter to taste, but the end is sweeter than honey.

   The writing in *Rain* says:

   > Who does not feel happy
   > When it begins to rain?
   > It is a very sure sign
   > That we shall have food.

   Discuss what these writings mean. Then write for ten minutes about one of the sayings (or you can write about another saying that you know). Is it true? Does the saying relate to your own life?

2. Describe your home. Where is it? What is in it? Do you like your home? Why or why not?

CHAPTER **three**

Living to Eat or Eating to Live?

Traditional food for the holiday kwansaa

in this chapter

You will write a paragraph about the special foods you eat for a holiday.

STEPS TO **writing**

1. Exploring Ideas
Describing Holiday Foods

 Discuss the picture below. What are the people doing? What do you think they are eating?

 Write in your journal about typical everyday meals in your country. Write as much as possible in about five minutes. Don't worry about form or grammar.

exercise 3 Discuss your entry with other students. Make a list of the different kinds of food from the discussion. If you don't know the name of a food, describe it. Maybe your teacher or other students can help you.

example: POPULAR FOODS

Name   Description
tacos   fried corn pancakes with meat and salad filling

exercise 4 Look at this list of dishes for the American holiday, Thanksgiving. Then think of the food you eat on a holiday in your home country. Make a list of the special dishes. Sometimes there is no English word for a special dish from your home country. Write the word in your language and explain it. The first one is done as an example.

Holiday: _Thanksgiving_____   stuffing_____

turkey_____   sweet potatoes_____

cranberry sauce_____   pumpkin pie_____

Your Holiday: _____   _____

_____   _____

_____   _____

exercise 5 Write some sentences that compare the special food you eat on holidays with the food you eat every day.

example: People usually prepare and eat more food on Thanksgiving. The Thanksgiving meal is more delicious than our everyday meals.

_____

_____

_____

_____

_____

_____

_____

Three generations at
Thanksgiving dinner

Chapter Three • Living to Eat or Eating to Live?   **33**

Building Vocabulary

 **exercise 6** Work in small groups. Look at the sentences you wrote about the special foods you eat on holidays. What vocabulary is new to you? Add your words to the chart below. Some words are there as examples.

NOUNS	VERBS	ADJECTIVES	OTHER
celebration	celebrate	joyous	_____
feast	feast on	traditional	_____
dish	_____	typical	_____
_____	_____	_____	_____
_____	_____	_____	_____
_____	_____	_____	_____
_____	_____	_____	_____

2. Organizing Ideas
Ordering Information in a Paragraph

People often begin a paragraph with general ideas and then write more specific ones. The last sentence of a paragraph often describes a personal reaction, opinion, or feeling. For example, here are some notes about Thanksgiving:

1. Thanksgiving is a family celebration to remember the first harvest of American colonists.

2. People eat traditional foods from the first Thanksgiving feast.

3. Some typical Thanksgiving foods are turkey, stuffing, sweet potatoes, homemade bread, and pies.

4. People eat more than usual on Thanksgiving, but they feel full and happy.

 Organize these sentences into the correct order. Number them from 1, for the first in order, to 7, for the last.

1. _____ Everyone eats more than usual, and at the end of the day we are as stuffed (full) as the turkey.

2. _____ In my family, everyone brings a special dish for the Thanksgiving meal.

3. _____ My aunt bakes a turkey and fills it with stuffing, a mixture of bread and spices.

4. _____ Thanksgiving is a family celebration.

5. _____ They prepare many traditional foods such as turkey, sweet potatoes, and cranberry sauce.

6. _____ On this day Americans remember the first Thanksgiving feast of the early American colonists.

7. _____ My relatives also make bread, vegetables, salad, and at least four pies.

 Make similar notes for your paragraph. Answer these questions in your notes.

1. What's the name of the holiday? What does it celebrate?
2. Why do people eat special dishes on this holiday?
3. What does your family eat on the holiday?
4. How do you feel about the holiday?

Writing Topic Sentences

The topic sentence:

- gives the main idea of the paragraph.
- is always a complete sentence and has a subject and a verb.
- is often the first sentence in a paragraph but is sometimes the second or even the last sentence.

 Which of these main ideas about Thanksgiving are complete sentences? Write a C in front of the complete sentences.

1. _____ The Thanksgiving meal is a special celebration.

2. _____ Thanksgiving, an important celebration.

3. _____ Families eat typical American dishes on Thanksgiving.

4. _____ A Thanksgiving feast for a family celebration.

5. _____ Thanksgiving is an important American holiday.

exercise 4　Look at the sentences about the Thanksgiving meal in Exercise 1. Which sentence is the topic sentence? Underline it.

exercise 5　Look at the notes you wrote for your paragraph. First, decide if you want to add or change anything. Then write a topic sentence for your paragraph. Remember, it may be the first or second sentence in your paragraph. Exchange your notes and your topic sentence with a partner and answer these questions:

1. Is the topic sentence a complete sentence?
2. Does it give the main idea that was in your partner's notes?

3. Developing Cohesion and Style

Count and Noncount Nouns

There are two kinds of nouns in English: count and noncount nouns. Here are some examples.

	examples		notes
	Singular	**Plural**	
Count Nouns	a meal an egg one roll a turkey* a potato	three meals some eggs a few rolls many turkeys potatoes	Singular count nouns often have *a, an,* or *one* before them. Plural count nouns can have numbers or expressions of quantity† before them. Most plural count nouns have *-s* or *-es* endings.
Noncount Nouns	butter juice turkey* some salt a little sugar much food		Some expressions of quantity can be used before noncount nouns but <u>not</u> *a, an,* or numbers. Noncount nouns have no plural forms. In English, most noncount nouns describe whole things (or groups of things) made up of smaller or different parts, such as *meat, salt, food, or juice.*

*Some nouns can be used as a count noun or as a noncount noun. For example:
　How many *turkeys* are you going to buy? (count)
　I love to eat *turkey* on Thanksgiving. (noncount)
†Some expressions of quantity are: *some, a few, a lot of, a little, much, many.*

 exercise **1** Look at the list of food items you wrote in Exercise 4 on page 33. In small groups, discuss which items on your list are count nouns and which are noncount nouns. Put a √ after the noncount nouns.

Giving Examples with *such as*

When you write, you can introduce examples with the phrase *such as.*

example: On Thanksgiving Day we eat many traditional foods. The foods are turkey, sweet potatoes, and cranberries. →
On Thanksgiving Day we eat many traditional foods *such as turkey, sweet potatoes, and cranberries.*

 exercise **2** How well do you know ethnic food? Look at the list of ethnic dishes. In small groups, discuss what the different dishes are. Then write the name of each dish under the correct heading as in the example.

example:　A: Who knows what ravioli is?
B: It's a kind of Italian food.
C: Right. It's a kind of small, square pasta. It's filled with cheese or meat.

- dim sum
- tacos
- samosas
- ravioli

- enchiladas
- spring rolls
- curry
- cannoli

- tamales
- mulligatawny soup
- minestrone soup
- moo shu pork

ITALIAN	CHINESE	MEXICAN	INDIAN
ravioli	_____	_____	_____
_____	_____	_____	_____
_____	_____	_____	_____

Now write sentences with *such as*. The first sentence is done for you.

1. Italian restaurants serve many wonderful dishes such as ravioli, cannoli, and minestrone soup.

2. In Chinese restaurants you can try delicious dishes _____
_____

3. _____
_____

4. _____
_____

Look at your list of nouns from Building Vocabulary on page 34. Can you use *such as* to give examples of any of the nouns? Write a sentence with *such as*. Then compare it to sentences by other students.

_____

_____

Using Appositives

When you talk about typical native dishes, you sometimes have to explain what they are. You can use an appositive to explain them. A comma goes before the explanation. If the explanation is not at the end of the sentence, another comma goes after it.

examples: Turkey stuffing is a traditional Thanksgiving food. Stuffing is a mixture of bread and spices. →
Turkey <u>stuffing</u>, *a mixture of bread and spices,* is a traditional Thanksgiving food.

My mother fills the turkey with stuffing. Stuffing is a mixture of bread and spices. →
My mother fills the turkey with <u>stuffing</u>, *a mixture of bread and spices.*

exercise 5   Use appositives to combine these sentences.

1. A typical Middle Eastern dish is falafel. Falafel is a mixture of fried chick peas and spices. _____

_____

2. We like to eat dim sum. Dim sum is a Chinese meal of dumplings and other small, delicious kinds of food. _____

_____

3. People like to eat tempura. Tempura is a Japanese dish of fried shrimp and vegetables. _____

_____

_____

4. A favorite dish is chicken fesenjan. Chicken fesenjan is chicken in a spicy pomegranate sauce. _____

_____

Can you explain any of the typical dishes for your holiday using appositives? Write a sentence with an appositive. Then compare it to sentences by other students.

_____

_____

4. Writing the First Draft

Write your paragraph. Include the name of the holiday in your title, such as in the title "A Thanksgiving Meal." Use the topic sentence and your notes. Try to use *such as* and appositives in your paragraph.

5. Editing Practice
Using Commas with Appositives

Commas separate an appositive from the rest of a sentence.

example: On February 14, many people send valentines, cards that say "I love you."

My mother makes pfeffernuesse, a spicy German cookie, for Christmas.

Add commas to these sentences.

1. Rijsttafel an Indonesian rice and curry dish is popular in Amsterdam.
2. Americans often eat hot dogs pork or beef sausages on the Fourth of July.
3. For breakfast I like to eat blintzes pancakes with a cheese filling.
4. My friend makes great bouillabaisse a French fish soup.
5. Spaghetti an Italian noodle dish is popular in North America.

Forming Noun Plurals

Write the correct plural forms of these nouns. (See Appendix One, pages 174 and 175, for spelling rules.)

1. cookie_____   3. peach _____

2. orange _____   4. tomato _____

5. dish _____   **8.** knife_____

6. pancake _____   **9.** serving _____

7. cherry _____   **10.** box _____

Spelling Third-Person Singular Verbs

Write the correct third-person singular forms of these verbs. (See Appendix One, pages 174 and 175, for spelling rules.)

1. He (miss) _____   **6.** He (mix) _____

2. She (watch) _____   **7.** She (play) _____

3. He (cook) _____   **8.** It (wash) _____

4. It (eat) _____   **9.** He (drink) _____

5. She (hurry) _____   **10.** She (dry) _____

exercise **4**

Edit this paragraph twice. First, find a place to add *such as* before examples. The second time check to see if the count and noncount nouns are correct. Make any other changes you think are necessary.

SPECIAL CHRISTMAS FOODS

Christmas is an important holiday for many people in the United States. It is the celebration of the birth of Christ. People in North America prepare many special Christmas food from all over the world. Many Christmas specialties fruitcake and eggnog come from Great Britain. North Americans make fruitcakes with fruits, nuts, and liquors. Eggnog is a drink of eggs, milks, and sometimes rum. American also eat a lot of Christmas cookies. I love all the special Christmas food.

6. Editing Your Writing

 Edit your letter using the following checklist.

Editing Checklist

1. Content
   a. Is the paragraph interesting?
   b. Is the information clear?
2. Organization
   a. Does the topic sentence give the main idea of the paragraph? Is it a complete sentence?
   b. Are all the sentences about the holiday?
   c. Are the sentences in logical order?
3. Cohesion and Style
   a. Can you connect any sentences with *and, so,* or *but*?
   b. Are the appositives correct?
   c. Does *such as* introduce examples?
4. Grammar
   a. Are the present-tense verbs correct?
   b. Are the count and noncount nouns correct?
5. Form
   a. Is the paragraph form (indentation, capitalization, and punctuation) correct?
   b. Is the spelling of words with *-s* endings correct?
   c. Is the use of commas with appositives correct?

 Show your paper to another student. Does he or she understand your paragraph? Does he or she think you need to make any other corrections?

7. Writing the Second Draft

Write the second draft of your paragraph using neat handwriting and correct form. Then give it to your teacher for comments.

When your teacher returns your paragraph, look at her or his comments. If you don't understand something, ask about it. Then make a list of things you do well and the things you need to work on.

What I do well:

1. _____

_____

_____

2. _____

_____

_____

3. _____

_____

_____

What I need to work on:

1. _____

_____

_____

2. _____

_____

_____

3. _____

_____

_____

WHAT DO YOU THINK?

We often use words that describe foods to describe people's personalities:

- warm/cold
- sweet/sour
- spicy/bland
- salty/peppery
- natural/artificial

1. Discuss these words in small groups. What kinds of foods do they describe? What kinds of people do they describe?
2. In English we have a saying: "You are what you eat." In other cultures too, people say that different kinds of foods change people in different ways. For example, some Chinese say that there are "yang" and "yin" foods. Yang foods give people energy, and yin foods make them tired. Do people in your home country group foods in different ways? Do they say that the food you eat can change how you act or feel? Do you think that this is true or not? Write about what you think for ten minutes in your journal. Exchange your entries in small groups and discuss what you think.

A STEP beyond

Try to find pictures of the holiday celebration you describe in your paragraph. Bring family pictures or pictures from books to class. In small groups, read your paragraphs aloud and show each other the pictures you have.

When something is very American, Americans say it is "as American as apple pie." This is because apple pie is one of North Americans' favorite foods. Look at the recipe for apple pie. Then write a recipe for one of your favorite holiday dishes. Collect all the recipes. If possible, copy them and make a recipe booklet for each student in the class. You may also want to have a party; if so, invite everyone to bring their favorite dish.

Sifting flour

Cutting in butter
with a pastry blender

Rolling out dough

Covering pie with dough

APPLE PIE

Preheat oven to 450°F (232°C)

2 cups flour
1 teaspoon salt
2/3 cup butter, margarine or shortening
1/4 cup water

5 to 6 cups apples
1/3 to 2/3 cup white or brown sugar
1/8 teaspoon salt
1 to 1 1/2 tablespoons cornstarch
1/4 teaspoon cinnamon
1 1/2 tablespoons butter

Sift the flour and salt into a bowl. Then resift. Put 1/3 of this mixture into another bowl
and stir in the water. Cut the butter or shortening into the flour mixture in the first bowl
(use two knives or a pastry blender), until the pieces are the size of peas. Stir in the
flour and water mixture and make into a ball with your hands. Roll out half and put it
into a pie pan.

Peel, core and cut the apples into thin pieces. Combine the sugar, salt, cornstarch and
cinnamon and mix with the apples. Put them into the pie pan with small pieces of butter.
Cover the pie with the other half of the dough.

Bake in a 450°F (232°C) oven for 10 minutes. Decrease the heat to 350°F (177°C) and bake
for another 35 to 50 minutes more.

Adapted from *Joy of Cooking*, Irma S. Rombauer and Marion Rombauer Becker. Indianapolis: Bobbs
Merrill, 1931.

 Find a classmate from another country or another part of your country, if possible. Together, choose a special occasion you both celebrate, such as a wedding or birthday party. Individually write about how you each celebrate it. What do you do? What do you eat? After you write your paragraphs, exchange them. How are your celebrations the same? How are they different?

Journal Writing

 Write in your journal for ten minutes about one or more of the following topics.

1. Why I love (or hate) holidays (or a particular holiday)
2. My favorite food
3. What I miss most about my country
4. My favorite restaurant or café

CHAPTER **four**

Getting Around the Community

in this chapter

You will write a letter to a friend who is coming to visit you. You will tell her or him some things you might do when she or he comes. You will also give directions to your home.

47

STEPS TO **writing**

1. Exploring Ideas

Describing Places, Things to Do, and Directions

 Write for ten minutes about your city or town. What's fun to do or see? What do you like or not like about it?

      example: In my city, there are many theaters . . .

Building Vocabulary

 Complete this chart with places your friend might like to visit or things she or he might like to do. Write as many places and things as you can.

PLACES TO VISIT

1. _____
2. _____
3. _____

4. _____
5. _____
6. _____

THINGS TO DO

INSIDE

1. _____
2. _____
3. _____

OUTSIDE

1. _____
2. _____
3. _____

 Compare your list with other students' lists. Are there any things you want to add or change?

exercise  Your friend is going to drive to your home. Look at a map of your town or city. Will your friend have to take a highway? If so, how will she or he get from the highway to your home? Are there any important landmarks (such as a lake, tall building, park, etc.) to help her or him? Draw a map that shows the route from the highway to your home. Label all the important streets. Include any important landmarks.

2. Organizing Ideas
Organizing Paragraphs in a Letter

> Your letter will have three paragraphs. Each paragraph has a different purpose.
>
> • The first paragraph will say hello, discuss the visit, and describe some of the activities you and your friend might do.
>
> • The second paragraph will give directions to your home.
>
> • The last paragraph will have only one or two sentences. The purpose of this paragraph is to say good-bye and end the letter.

exercise Look at the following sentences. Decide if they belong in paragraph 1, 2, or 3. Write 1, 2, or 3 on the line before each sentence.

a. _____ We can also go to a baseball game.

b. _____ There's a gas station on the corner.

c. _____ There's a concert at the City Auditorium.

d. _____ Make a left turn on Maple Avenue.

e. _____ Please write and tell me what time you will arrive.

f. _____ It won't be hard to find my house.

g. _____ It won't be easy to get theater tickets.

h. _____ I'm glad to hear that you are doing well.

i. _____ See you in two weeks.

3. Developing Cohesion and Style

Using Correct Verb Forms

exercise 1  Complete the sentences with the correct forms of the verbs in parentheses. Use the simple form, the present or future tense, or *be going to*.

There _____ (be) many things to do here. I'm sure that we

_____ (have) a good time. It will probably _____ (be hot),

so _____ (bring) your bathing suit. There _____ (be a beach)

very near my home. I _____ (know)

you like music, and the London Symphony

_____ (give) a concert on Saturday

night. On Sunday we can _____ (visit)

the art museum or go hiking in Butler

State Park.

Using Prepositions

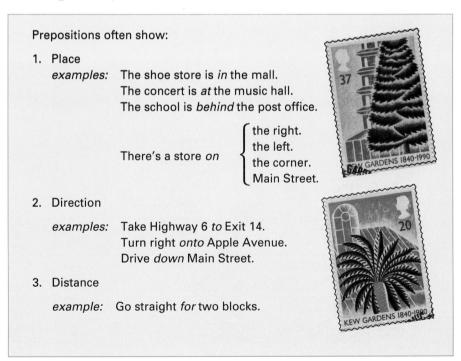

Prepositions often show:

1. Place

   examples: The shoe store is *in* the mall.
   The concert is *at* the music hall.
   The school is *behind* the post office.

   There's a store *on* { the right.
   the left.
   the corner.
   Main Street. }

2. Direction

   examples: Take Highway 6 *to* Exit 14.
   Turn right *onto* Apple Avenue.
   Drive *down* Main Street.

3. Distance

   example: Go straight *for* two blocks.

exercise 2 — Underline the prepositions of place, direction, and distance in the following paragraph. Then exchange papers with another student and compare them.

Take Route 44 south to Exit 12. Turn right at the first light. You will be on Maple Avenue. Go straight down Maple Avenue for two miles. At the corner of Bryant and Maple you will see an elementary school. Turn right at the first street after the school. The name of the street is Roosevelt Drive. Go straight for five blocks. Then make a left turn onto Broadmoor. My apartment building isn't difficult to find. It's on the left, Number 122. You can park your car behind the building.

exercise 3 — Complete the paragraph with the prepositions below. There may be more than one possible answer.

at   on   in   to   for

Turn right _____ Smith's Drugstore. You will be _____
1   2

Church Street. Go straight _____ Church _____ two
3   4

blocks. Then turn left _____ the corner of Church and Findlay.
5

Go straight _____ one block. Then turn left _____
6   7

Hudson Drive. My house is the third one _____ the left.
8

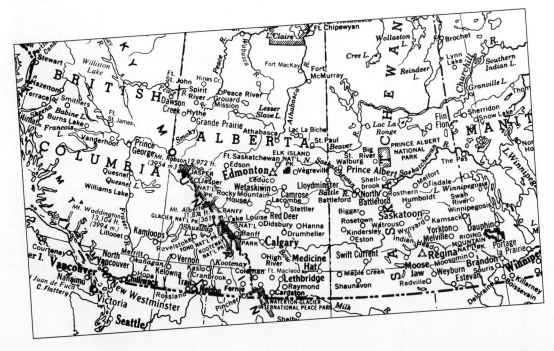

exercise 4  Look at the following map. Work with a partner. One student will write directions from the post office to the library. The other student will write directions from the supermarket to the park. Exchange papers. Can you understand your partner's directions? Make any necessary corrections.

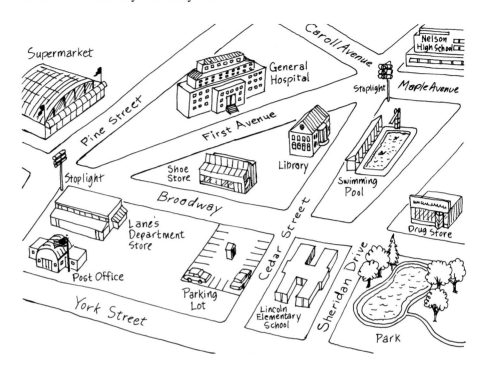

Using *there* and *it*

exercise 5 Look at these two sentences.

There is a supermarket on the corner. *It* has a big red and white sign.

The word *it* is a pronoun. It replaces a noun in a sentence. The word *there* does not replace a noun in a sentence. In the sentence above, what noun does *it* replace?

exercise 6 Complete the following paragraph with *there* or *it*.

_____ are many things to see in Washington. _____ is a
    1   2

very interesting city. In the center of the city _____ is a large
                                                   3

open area. People call _____ the mall. All around the mall
                         4

_____ are museums. In the center of the mall _____ is a
    5   6

very large structure. _____ is the Washington Monument.
                        7

4. Writing the First Draft

Write the letter to your friend. In the first paragraph, describe what you are going to do during her or his visit. In the second paragraph, give directions to your home. In the third paragraph, say good-bye and tell your friend how excited you are about the visit.

5. Editing Practice
Using Correct Form in an Informal Letter

This is one example of an informal letter.

Date   July 12, 19XX

Salutation
Dear Bill,

> I am excited about your visit. There's a lot to do here, and I'm sure we'll have a great time. On Saturday afternoon we can go to a basketball game. I think I can get tickets. In the evening we're going to go to Randy's house for dinner. After dinner we might go to a rock concert. I'm going to try to get tickets. If you want, on Sunday we can play tennis in the morning and visit the planetarium in the afternoon.
> It's easy to find my house. Just take the Connecticut Turnpike east to Exit 5. Turn left at the first light. Then you will be on Bradford Boulevard. Go straight on Bradford for three miles. Then turn left on Apple. You will see a large supermarket on your left. Go to the second light. Make a right turn on Woodgate Road. My building is on the right, three houses from the corner. It's number 417.
> See you in two weeks.

Body

Closing   Sincerely,

Steve

Date   The date usually appears in the upper right-hand corner. The order of the date is month, day, year. Capitalize the name of the month and put a comma after the day and before the year. Do not use a comma in the year.

example: April 4, 19XX

Salutation   Most letters begin with *Dear.* Use the name that you usually call the person. In an informal letter a comma goes after the name.

example: Dear Professor Hudson,
           Dear Dr. Fitzgerald,
           Dear Mr. and Mrs. White,
           Dear Melinda,

Body   Indent each paragraph of the letter. In letters, paragraphs may have only one or two sentences. Although it is important to write each paragraph on a different topic, the paragraphs in a letter do not always begin with a topic sentence.

Closing   The closing of a letter begins either at the left or in the center of the page. There are many different closings. The closing that you choose depends on your relationship with the person you are writing to.

example: Regards,
           Best wishes, } for informal letters

           Fondly,
           Love, } for letters to close friends or relatives

 *exercise 1*   Edit this letter using the editing checklist on page 11, Chapter One. Then rewrite the letter using correct letter form.

June 15, 19XX

Dear Mary, I'm very glad that you visit me next week. We will to have a good time. It's easy to find my house. Make left turn at the corner of Broadway and Fifth Street. Drive down Fifth two blocks. Make a right turn on Henry Street. There are a park on the corner. My house is on the left side. It are number 150. the weather is warm so we might going hiking and swimming. Please to bring your photo album. I want see the pictures of your family.

Addressing An Envelope

This is the correct way to address an envelope.

Carol Martin
128 Lake Drive, Apt. 8
Muskegon, Michigan 49441
U.S.A.

Return Address

Zip Code

Stamp

Address

Mr. and Mrs. Daniel Kaufman
432 St. George Street
Toronto, Ontario
CANADA M56 2V8

Postal Code

Return Address Write your address in the top left-hand corner of the envelope.

Address Write the address clearly. You may want to print it. Make sure the address is complete. If there is an apartment number, be sure to include it. It is also important to use the **zip code** or the **postal code**.

 *exercise* **2**   Address an envelope for the letter on page 54. Write your name and address as the return address. Then correct this address and write it on the envelope below.

Mary pirewali, 256 rose avenue, san jose 519478 calif united states.

6. Editing Your Writing

 exercise **1** Edit your letter using the following checklist.

Editing Checklist

1. Content
   a. Are the activities interesting?
   b. Are the directions clear?
2. Organization
   Is each paragraph about a different topic?
3. Cohesion and style
   a. Are the prepositions correct?
   b. Is the use of *there* and *it* correct?
4. Grammar
   Are the verb forms correct?
5. Form
   a. Is the date correct?
   b. Is the salutation correct?
   c. Do the paragraphs begin with an indentation?
   d. Is the closing in the right place?

exercise **2** Exchange letters with another student. Discuss the letters. Are there any other changes you should make?

7. Writing the Second Draft

Write the second draft of your letter using neat handwriting and correct form. Then give the letter to your teacher for comments. When your teacher returns your letter, ask him or her about any comments you don't understand. Is there any improvement in your writing?

WHAT DO YOU THINK?

Evaluating Community Services

1. Discuss the types of services and assistance that are available in your school or community. (Examples are health programs, children's services, public transportation, job information, and recreation programs.) You can go to your school or neighborhood library and ask the librarian for information about services available nearby. What services are especially important for foreign students and newcomers to a community? Are there any services in your school or community that you or your family use? Are the services good or bad? What other services should be available?

2. Write for fifteen minutes about a service you use or would like to use. Describe the service and tell why it is or is not helpful.

A STEP beyond

 Exchange letters with another student. Can you understand the directions? Try to draw a map from the highway to your partner's home. Then pretend you are the friend and write a reply. Thank your friend for the letter and say you are excited about going. Ask any questions you may have about the visit or the directions.

 Write another letter to a friend who speaks English. Describe what you are doing these days. Say what you like and don't like about your life.

 You want to invite a friend from school to your home. Write her or him an invitation note. Explain in your note how to get from school to your home. Draw a small map.

Journal Writing

 Write for ten or fifteen minutes about one or both of these topics.

1. Compare the place you are now living with a place you lived before. Describe the places. Which one do you like best? Why?

2. Write about your community's transportation. How do people generally get around? Is the transportation good or bad?

CHAPTER five

Home

You will write a paragraph about a part of your life.

1. Exploring Ideas

Using a Lifeline

Draw a line down the middle of a piece of paper. The top of the line represents the year you were born, and the bottom of the line is the present time. You can write some ages along the line too, as in the picture on page 61. Think about your life and write some of the important events on the left of the lifeline. Write your feelings about your life on the right. Write in English if possible, but don't worry about correctness. If you can't think of something in English, use your native language. You can use pictures and symbols, and you may also want to look at family photographs. Look at the woman's lifeline on page 61 as an example.

Building Vocabulary

Did you need to write any words or phrases in your native language? Look them up in a dictionary and write their meanings in English. Then write a sentence that uses each new word or phrase. Show your sentences to the other students in your group. Do they think you used the words correctly? Ask your teacher to check your sentences.

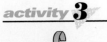

Show your lifeline to some other students and talk about your life. Ask each other questions. What do the other students think is interesting about your life?

2. Organizing Ideas
Limiting Information

> You can't write about your whole life in one paragraph, so you need to choose one part of your life to write about. You may want to write about your childhood, your school years, or one important event in your life.

 Look at the woman's lifeline again. Discuss where a paragraph on a part of her life can begin and end.

 Now look at your own lifeline and choose a part of your life to write about. As you think about the different parts, consider the following points.

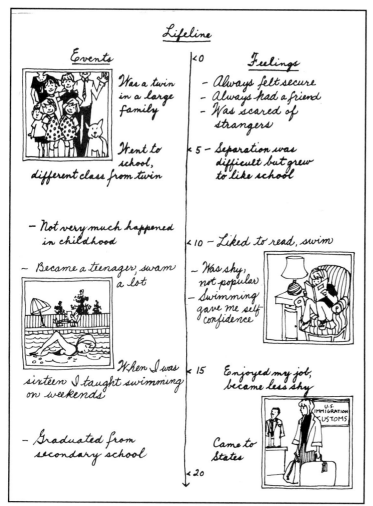

- Is this part of my life interesting? Often unusual or funny events are more interesting to write about.

- Is this part of my life important?

- Is this part of my life about one topic? Don't try to write about too many events or times.

Everything in your paragraph should be about one main subject.

Discuss your decision with some other classmates. Do they agree with your choice?

Making Paragraph Notes

Look at the part of the lifeline you chose and add information you think is important. Cross out information that is not about the topic of your paragraph.

Writing Topic Sentences

exercise 3

Look at these paragraph notes. For each paragraph, circle the number of the topic sentence that you think gives the main idea. Discuss your choices with your classmates.

PARAGRAPH 1

- was born a twin—very important to childhood
- large family
- always had a friend, felt secure
- separation from twin sister at school was difficult

TOPIC SENTENCES

1. Because I was born a twin, I had a very different childhood from most people.
2. Because I had a twin sister, I felt secure.
3. I didn't like school because I was in different classes from my twin sister.

PARAGRAPH 2

- teenage years difficult
- liked to read, was shy, not popular
- was a good swimmer
- taught swimming on weekends
- this gave me self-confidence

TOPIC SENTENCES

1. I wasn't popular as a teenager.
2. As a teenager, I taught swimming on weekends.
3. My teenage years were very difficult at first, but they ended happily.

exercise 4

Write a topic sentence that gives the main idea for your paragraph. Show the notes for your paragraph and your topic sentence to other students. Do they think you need to change anything?

_____

_____

Writing Titles

The title should give the main idea of a composition. It should also be interesting. It goes on the top line of the paper and is not a complete sentence.

In the title, capitalize the first word and all the important words. Don't capitalize the following kinds of words (unless they're the first word in the title):

- conjunctions: *and, but, or, so*
- articles: *the, a, an*
- short prepositions: *at, by, for, in, of, on, out, to, up, with*

 Write these titles with the correct capitalization.

1. an exciting life _____

2. all's well that ends well _____

3. a gift of hope _____

4. the best years of my life _____

5. going away _____

6. a happy ending _____

7. life in a new city _____

8. best friends _____

9. a new beginning _____

10. a wonderful experience _____

 Look at the possible titles for the paragraphs about the twin. Put a checkmark by the titles that you like. Why do you like them?

PARAGRAPH **1**

My childhood
Born a Twin
Difficult School Years
My childhood as a Twin

PARAGRAPH **2**

Growing Up
Unhappy Teens
Teenage Years
Teaching Swimming

 Look at your paragraph notes and write a title for your paragraph.

_____

3. Developing Cohesion and Style
Using the Past Tense

> Because you are writing about events in the past, most of your sentences will be in the past tense.

exercise **1**   Complete the following paragraph with the correct past-tense forms of the verbs in parentheses. For the spelling of verbs with -*ed,* see Appendix One, page 174, at the back of this book.

Because I _____ (be) born a twin, I _____ (have) a
        1   2
very different childhood from most people. There _____ (be)
                                                                    3
always someone to play with and I always _____ (have) a friend.
                                                              4
My mother said we _____ (feed) each other, _____ (play)
                          5   6
together, and _____ (cry) when strangers came near. We
                      7
_____ (do) everything together. When my sister
        8
_____ (need) special shoes, I _____ (want) them too.
        9   10
But life as a twin _____ (not be) always great. My mother
                            11
_____ (be) always tired because she _____ (work) so
        12   13
hard. My father _____ (say) he _____ (hate) to come
                          14   15
home because with my older brother there _____ (be) three
                                                              16
screaming babies in the house. Even now I think that when I get something

I want, someone else will go without.

exercise **2**   Look at your paragraph notes and write sentences with past-tense verbs about your life. Compare your verbs with those of other students. Can you use any of their words? Also be careful to use past-tense verbs only for completed events; don't write "I studied English for three years" if you are still studying English.

_____

_____

_____

_____

_____

Combining Sentences with Time Words and *because*

> - When you write a paragraph that describes events, you can use time words to combine sentences. Some common time words are *before, after, when,* and *as soon as.*
>
>   examples: *Before* I started school, I was very happy.
>   *After* I left high school, I got a job.
>   *When* my family said good-bye, I was very sad.
>   *As soon as* I came to the United States, I got sick.
>
> - You can also combine sentences with *because* to show reasons.
>
>   example: *Because* she worked hard, my mother was always tired.
>
> - To review how to combine sentences with *and, but,* or *so,* see Chapter One.

 Complete the following paragraph with *before, after, when, as soon as, because, and, but,* or *so.*

I had a typical childhood. _____ my life changed _____
                                       1   2
I was fourteen. We moved from our small village to Karachi, a big city in Pakistan. _____ we moved, life in the country was wonderful for
                       3
me, but _____ I started school in Karachi, I became shy and
                 4
nervous. The other boys in my classes were tough. _____ they
                                            5
laughed at my country ways. _____ I didn't like the other boys, I
                             6
became more interested in books. I always liked biology, _____ I
                                               7
started to read about medicine. I was very unhappy at the time,
_____ I'm glad this happened _____ I finally decided to
         8   9
become a doctor.

1. When I became a teenager, I _____

   _____

2. I came to this country because _____

   _____

3. When I was a child, I _____

   _____

4. After I left high school, I _____

   _____

5. Before I started this class, _____

   _____

6. I wasn't very happy, but _____

   _____

 Write at least two sentences about your life, using the information in your paragraph notes. Use *because, before, after, when,* or *as soon as.* Use correct punctuation. _____

_____

_____

4. Writing the First Draft

Now write your paragraph about a part of your life. Use the topic sentence and the notes you wrote. Combine some sentences with time words and *because, and, but,* and *so.* Remember to use the past tense when you write about completed actions.

5. Editing Practice
Punctuating Sentences with Dependent Clauses

- When you add a time word or *because* to a sentence, it becomes a dependent clause. A dependent clause is not a complete sentence—it is a sentence fragment.

> *examples:* When I was five.
> Because my father had a new job. } *sentence fragments*
>
> You must combine a dependent clause with an independent clause—
> a clause that is a complete sentence by itself.
>
> • If the dependent clause appears at the beginning of a sentence, use a
> comma after it.
>
> *examples:* When I was five, we moved to Caracas.
> Because my father had a new job, we moved to Caracas.
>
> • If the dependent clause appears at the end of the sentence, don't use a
> comma in front of it.
>
> *examples:* We moved to Caracas when I was five.
> We moved to Caracas because my father had a new job.

 **exercise 1**

Some of these sentences have correct punctuation and some don't. Write *correct*
after the sentence if the punctuation is correct. Rewrite the sentence with correct
punctuation if it is wrong.

1. *Before* we moved here we used to have many friends and relatives

nearby. _____

_____

_____

2. *Because* my uncle was an engineer, he sent me to engineering school.

_____

_____

3. I left the farm, *as soon as* I could _____

_____

4. We moved to Colorado. *Because* the doctors said I needed a dry climate.

_____

_____

5. *When* I first came here, I loved the excitement of New York. _____

_____

6. I came to the city, *when* I was five. _____

_____

 **exercise 2** Edit this paragraph twice and rewrite it correctly. The first time, see where you can combine sentences with *and, but,* and *so.* (Remember to use correct punctuation.) The second time, correct past-tense verb forms. Make any other changes you think are necessary.

HOW I BECAME A JAZZ MUSICIAN

   I fall in love with jazz when I am five years old. I always heared jazz in the streets but for my fifth birthday my brother tooks me to a concert. There I saw a great saxophonist I decided to learn to play the saxophone. First I need a saxophone, I ask my father. My father say he no have money for a saxophone. I work for my brother, uncles, and cousins. I made a little money then my father see I work hard. He gave me money for a saxophone. I listen to recordings. My brother teach me. I practice every day. Soon I am a good saxophone player.

6. Editing Your Writing

 **exercise 1** Edit your paragraph using the following checklist.

Editing Checklist

1. Content
   a. Is the information interesting?
   b. Is the information important?
   c. Is there an interesting title?
2. Organization
   a. Does the topic sentence give the main idea of the paragraph?
   b. Are all the sentences about one topic?
   c. Should you change the order of any of the sentences?
3. Cohesion and Style
   Did you combine sentences with time words and *and, but, so,* and *because*?
4. Grammar
   a. Are your nouns, pronouns, and articles correct?
   b. Did you use good sentence structure (no sentence fragments)?
   c. Did you use the correct past-tense verbs?
5. Form
   a. Did you use correct paragraph form?
   b. Did you capitalize the words in the title correctly?
   c. Did you use correct punctuation when you combined sentences?

 **exercise 2** Exchange paragraphs with another student. Discuss the paragraphs. Are there any other changes you should make?

7. Writing the Second Draft

Rewrite your paragraph using neat handwriting and correct form. Then give it to your teacher for comments.

Using Feedback

exercise Look at your teacher's comments. If you don't understand something, ask about it. Then look at all the paragraphs you wrote before and the teacher's comments on them. Make a list of goals. Write down things you can do to improve your writing. Use these questions to help you write your goals.

1. Are your paragraphs interesting?
2. Are your ideas clear?
3. Are you organizing your paragraphs well?
4. Are you using good topic sentences?
5. Are there any grammatical structures you need to practice?
6. Do you need to use neater handwriting?
7. Is your spelling correct?
8. Are you using correct paragraph form?
9. How are your punctuation and capitalization?
10. Are you trying to write sentences that are too difficult?

WHAT DO YOU THINK?

Thinking About Birth Order

Many people believe that the birth order of children in a family affects the kind of people that they become. For example, people say that the eldest (first-born) child is often more independent and a better leader.

What do you think? What is your birth order in your family? Has it affected you? How? Write for ten minutes in your journal. Then discuss what you wrote with your classmates.

A STEP beyond

 **activity 1**

If you want, let other students read your paragraph. You may want to show them pictures of you and your family too. Discuss the experiences you wrote about. Did other students have similar experiences? Do you have questions about the other students' paragraphs?

 **activity 2**

Interview a friend or a relative about her or his life. Then choose one part and write about it.

 **activity 3**

Invent a life for yourself. Write about how you wish your life had been. Use the past tense.

> **example:** I was born into a very rich family. We lived in Venice for eight years. Then we moved to Florence.

Journal Writing

 **activity 4**

Write in your journal for ten minutes about one of the following topics.

1. The happiest time in my life
2. The saddest time in my life

CHAPTER six

Emergencies and Strange Experiences

in this chapter

You will write an ending to a mystery story.

STEPS TO **writing**

1. Exploring Ideas
Creating an Ending to a Story

exercise 1 Read this story.

It was a day just like any other day. Marvin got up when his alarm clock rang at seven o'clock. He smiled as he put on his uniform. Then he stood up straight and looked at himself in the mirror. He saw a short, slightly overweight man with a small moustache and a kind face. "At least the uniform looks good," he thought. He liked the blue uniform. When he put it on, he felt important.

Marvin listened to the news while he made breakfast in his tiny kitchen. The announcer was saying something about a convict who had escaped from prison, but Marvin wasn't paying attention. He was thinking about his father. His father was disappointed with him. Marvin knew that. But it wasn't his fault that he was too short to be a police officer.

After he finished his breakfast, Marvin prepared to leave for work. He washed his breakfast dishes, watered his plants, and fed his cat, Amelia. He arrived at work exactly on time. He always did.

There was a lot of mail that day. Before he could make his deliveries, he had to sort the letters and packages. When he finished, he put the mail into his large brown bag, put the bag on his shoulder, and left the post office.

One of his first stops was Dr. Jordan's house. As he was putting the mail into the mailbox, he heard a noise inside the house. "That's strange," he thought. "The Jordans are on vacation. They won't be home until tomorrow." He decided to go and look in the window.

Interactions I • Writing

 **2** In this chapter you are going to write the ending to this story. Before you write, you should think about Marvin. Look at these pictures. Which one do you think looks like Marvin?

exercise 3 Think about Marvin's personality. Answer these questions and give reasons for your answers.

1. Is he lonely? _____

_____

2. Is he confident? _____

_____

3. Is he happy? _____

_____

4. Is he neat?_____

_____

5. Is he responsible?_____

_____

6. Does he work hard? _____

_____

7. What can you tell about Marvin from his apartment? _____

_____

exercise 4 Make notes for an ending for the story, but do not write it yet. Use these questions as a guide.

1. What did Marvin see when he looked in the window?
2. What did he decide to do after he looked in the window?
3. Why did he decide to do this?
4. How did he feel?

Building Vocabulary

exercise 5

The chart below has examples of words you can use to discuss crime. In small groups, discuss the meaning of these words. What other words about crime can you add to the list? Ask your teacher for help if necessary.

NOUNS	VERBS	ADJECTIVES AND ADVERBS	OTHER
murderer	hit	strong	_____
gun	shoot	frightened	_____
convict	arrest	_____	_____
safe	steal	_____	_____
_____	break in	_____	_____
_____	_____	_____	_____
_____	_____	_____	_____
_____	_____	_____	_____

activity 6

You will write the ending to the story in the past tense. Do you know the past forms of all the verbs you want to use? Write the past forms of the verbs in your list above.

2. Organizing Ideas
Using a Time Sequence

> Writers use time words such as *before, after, as, when, while, then,* and *as soon as* to organize the information in a story.

exercise 1

Look at the story about Marvin again. Make a list of the time words. Compare your list with another student's. Are there any words you missed?

Limiting Information

> You must write your ending in one paragraph. The paragraph should have 100 to 150 words. It is important to limit what you want to say.

 Look at your notes. Tell your story to another student, and discuss these questions.

1. Is my ending too complicated or difficult for the reader to understand?
2. Did I include too much description?
3. Can I fit everything into one paragraph?

Writing a Title

> The title of a story should be interesting and not too general, but it should not tell the reader how the story will end.

 Which of the following do you think is a good title? Circle the number. Why do you think it's good?

1. Marvin Runs Away
2. The Murder of Marvin
3. A Big Day for a Little Man
4. Marvin Catches a Thief
5. Marvin the Mailman

 Give your story a title. You may use one of the above or make up your own.

3. Developing Cohesion and Style

Using *when, while,* and *as* with the Past Continuous and the Simple Past Tenses

- If you want to talk about two actions in the past and one action interrupts the other, use *when* to introduce the interrupting action.

  example: The robber was opening the safe *when* the police officer came in.

- Use *while* or *as* to introduce the action in progress, the action that *was happening.*

  examples: *While* the robber was opening the safe, the police officer came in.

  As the robber was opening the safe, the police officer came in.

- Use *while* or *as* to describe the two actions in progress at the same time.

  examples: One robber was opening the safe *while* the other one was watching for the police.

  Marvin listened to the radio *as* he ate breakfast.

- Use *when* if one action follows the other.

  example: *When* the police officer entered the house, he heard a noise.

 **exercise 1**   Combine these sentences with *when, while,* or *as.* More than one answer may be correct.

1. Marvin was looking in the window. Someone grabbed his arm. _____

   _____

2. The man grabbed his arm. Marvin started to fight. _____

   _____

3. A neighbor saw the fight. He called the police. _____

   _____

4. One robber was in the house stealing the jewelry. Marvin and the other robber were fighting. _____

_____

_____

5. Dr. Jordan gave Marvin a reward. He heard the story. _____

_____

exercise **2** Look at the notes for your story and write three sentences: one with *when,* one with *while,* and one with *as.* _____

_____

_____

_____

_____

_____

_____

Using *as soon as*

> Use *as soon as* to emphasize that one action happened immediately after another.
>
> *examples:* *As soon as* he saw the thief, he ran away.
> He ran away *as soon as* he saw the thief.

 Combine these sentences with *as soon as.*

1. The thief saw Marvin. He started to run. _____

   _____

2. Marvin called an ambulance. He saw the blood. _____

   _____

3. The police arrived. They arrested Marvin. _____

   _____

4. The neighbor ran outside. He heard the shot. _____

   _____

 Look at the notes for your story and write two sentences with *as soon as.*

Using *then*

> You can use *then* when you are narrating a story: By using *then,* you can make the time sequence clear and not repeat the same words. Compare:
>
> *examples:* I ran out of the house. After I ran out of the house, I saw a man in the street.
> I ran out of the house. *Then* I saw a man in the street.

 Rewrite these sentences using *then.*

1. She heard a shot. After she heard the shot, she called the police. _____

   _____

2. He ate breakfast. After he ate breakfast, he fed the cat. _____

   _____

3. He washed the dishes. After he washed the dishes, he went to work.

   _____

4. She looked in the window. After she looked in the window, she saw the thief. _____

Varying Time Words and Phrases

Now you have learned several different time words:

when   *while*   *as*   *before*   *after*   *then*   *as soon as*

Although these words do not have exactly the same meaning, you can use some of them in place of others.

examples: *When* he saw the thief, he called the police.
He called the police *as soon as* he saw the thief.
After he saw the thief, he called the police.
He saw the thief. *Then* he called the police.
He saw the thief *before* he called the police.

To make your writing more interesting, it is important to vary the words you use.

 **exercise 6** Complete the sentences with the time words listed in the box above.

Marvin put down his mailbag. _____ he tiptoed over to the window.

_____ (1) _____ he looked inside, he saw a man's shadow. _____ he had

_____(2)_____ (3)

to make a decision. Should he call the police or should he go into the house?

_____ he was thinking. Marvin heard two voices from inside the

_____(4)

house. There were *two* men! _____ he realized this, he knew he

_____(5)

couldn't go into the house alone, and he decided to go call the police.

_____ he could leave the window, he felt a hand on his arm.

_____(6)

Using Descriptive Words

An interesting story tells the reader more than just what happened. It also describes important people or places.

 **exercise 7** Underline the descriptive words and phrases in the story about Marvin on page 72. Then look at the notes for your paragraph. Add adjectives that describe the people and places.

Using Quotations

A good story also tells the reader what the characters are thinking.

- When you write exactly what someone said or thought, you use quotation marks. Use quotation marks in pairs. Use one set at the beginning of the quotation and one at the end.

- A quotation is always set off from the rest of the sentence by a comma, a question mark, or an exclamation point.

> *examples:* "I should call the police," Marvin thought.
> "Maybe," Marvin thought, "I should call the police."
> "Stop those men!" Marvin yelled.
> "Should I try to stop them?" Marvin asked himself.

 **exercise 8**   Look at these sentences. Put quotation marks in the correct places.

1. Marvin thought, Who are those men?
2. You should be a policeman, Marvin's father said.
3. Come out of there! Marvin yelled.
4. Do you have a gun? Marvin asked.

 **exercise 9**   Underline the sentences in the story about Marvin that tell you about Marvin's thoughts. Then look at the notes for your paragraph again. Write some thoughts for Marvin that you can include in your story.

4. Writing the First Draft

Now write your ending to the story about Marvin. Remember to follow these three guidelines:

1. Use time words where they are necessary.
2. Include descriptive words.
3. Use quotations.

5. Editing Practice
Using Editing Symbols

There are some common editing symbols that your teacher or your classmates may use. In Chapter One you learned about the caret (∧). Here are
some other symbols and examples of how they are used.

sp   *wrong spelling*
    He is a stu**dint** in Texas. → He is a student in Texas.

sf   *sentence fragment*
    When I was ten. We moved to New York. →
    When I was ten, we moved to New York.

/   *use lowercase (small letters)*
    The Thief ran out the door. → The thief ran out the door.

    take out this word, letter, or punctuation
    Sylvia sang a song, as she washed the dishes. →
    Sylvia sang a song as she washed the dishes.

o   *add punctuation here*
    The doctor arrived at ten o'clock → The doctor arrived at ten o'clock.

exercise 1 Rewrite these sentences.

1. The police of**icer** helped Marvin. _____

_____

2. Then/he went to the police station. _____

_____

3. When he arrived there. He saw Dr. Jordan _____

_____

4. While he was talking to the doctor Marvin came in. _____

_____

5. Marvin's father proud of him. _____

_____

 **exercise 2**   Edit this paragraph twice. The first time, check that all the information is really important. Are there any sentences you can take out? The second time, check that the writer has used time expressions correctly. Make any other changes you think are necessary.

Marvin saw a man, while he looked in the window. It was a small, rectangular window. As soon as he decided to go inside. He walk around to the back door. Before he opened the door. He looked in the back window. The back window was large Then he thought maybe the man had a gun. Marvin decided to call the police. Suddenly, he heard a woman scream. "There's a man looking in the kitchen window!" Before Marvin heard the voice he knew the answer to the mystery. Dr. Jordan and his family were home.

6. Editing Your Writing

 **exercise 1**   Edit your paragraph using the following checklist.

Editing Checklist

1. Content
   a. Is the story clear?
   b. Is all the information important?
2. Organization
   a. Did you use time words where necessary?
   b. Did you add a title?
3. Cohesion and Style
   a. Did you vary the time words and expressions?
   b. Did you include enough description?
   c. Did you use quotations?
4. Grammar
   a. Did you use the correct forms of the past tense?
   b. Did you use the correct forms of the present continuous tense?
   c. Did you use good sentence structure (no fragments)?
5. Form
   a. Did you use commas correctly?
   b. Did you use quotation marks correctly?

 **exercise 2** Exchange paragraphs with another student. Use editing symbols to edit each other's paragraphs. Discuss your paragraphs. Are there any other changes you should make?

7. Writing the Second Draft

Write the second draft of your paragraph using neat handwriting and correct form. Then give it to your teacher for comments.

WHAT DO YOU THINK?

Considering Career Choices

Parents often have ideas about the careers that their children should follow. Sometimes they feel disappointed if their children don't agree. Do you think that parents should encourage their children to follow certain careers? Does it help the children? How can it hurt them? Write for ten minutes in your journal. Then discuss what you wrote with your classmates.

A STEP beyond

 **activity 1** Read your ending to the other students in the class.

 **activity 2** Write the beginning of a story. Give it to a classmate. She or he will write the ending.

 Rewrite a story that you know. It can be a famous story. It can be from a book or a movie. You can change the story if you wish.

 Write a story based on your life. However, don't write it as your life. Write as if it happened to someone else.

Journal Writing

 Write for ten minutes about the strangest experience you have ever had.

Health

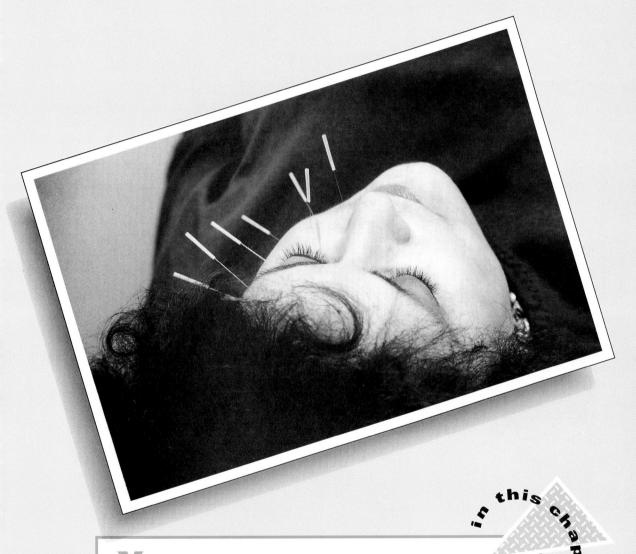

in this chapter

You will write a paragraph about the traditional treatments people in your home country sometimes use.

STEPS TO **writing**

1. Exploring Ideas

Discussing Modern and Traditional Remedies

exercise 1   Look at the pictures below and discuss them. What kinds of treatments are shown. What do you think of these treatments?

exercise 2   Discuss the following questions in small groups.

1. What do people in your home country do when they have colds? Do they usually take modern medicines? What traditional treatments do they use?
2. What do you do when you have a cold? Do you think modern treatments or traditional treatments are better?
3. What other traditional treatments do people in your country use? What do you think of them? Do the people in your group know about any similar treatments?

Building Vocabulary

 **exercise 3** The chart below has examples of vocabulary you can use to talk about health. What other new words can you add from your discussion? In small groups, discuss the meaning of any words you do not understand.

NOUNS	VERBS	ADJECTIVES	OTHER
treatment	treat	psychic	_____
acupuncture	heal	_____	_____
needles	take (medicine)	_____	_____
symptoms	massage	_____	_____
healer	relieve	_____	_____
_____	_____	_____	_____
_____	_____	_____	_____
_____	_____	_____	_____
_____	_____	_____	_____

2. Organizing Ideas
Making an Idea Map

 **exercise 1** To get your ideas on paper, make an "idea map." Write the words *Traditional Treatments* in the middle of a piece of paper. Then write all your ideas about that topic around the paper. Connect the ideas that go together. Look at the following example of an idea map of traditional treatments popular in the United States and Canada.

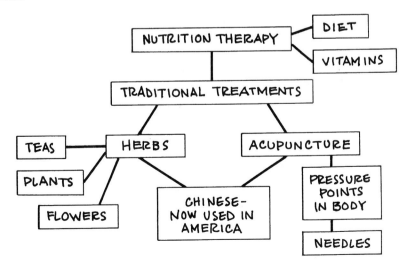

 Look at your idea map and make a list of the ideas you think would make a good paragraph. Use these questions to help you decide.

1. Is the information interesting?
2. Do you have enough information for a paragraph?
3. Can you limit the information to a single paragraph?
4. How do you want to organize your information? You can use one of the following suggestions, or your own idea.
   a. The different ways people use one kind of treatment
   b. The different treatments people use for one illness
   c. A short description of several different treatments you are familiar with

Writing Topic Sentences

 Circle the best topic sentence for a paragraph about herbs.

1. People often make teas with herbs to cure sore throats.
2. People in my country use herbs to treat many different diseases.
3. I don't think herbs are as good as modern medicines.

 Circle the best topic sentence for a paragraph about traditional treatments for colds.

1. You don't have to spend a lot of money at a pharmacy to treat a cold.
2. Lemon juice is a good traditional treatment for colds.
3. I had a horrible cold a year ago.

 Choose the best topic sentence for a paragraph about several different traditional treatments popular in the United States and Canada.

1. One traditional treatment people in the United States and Canada often use is massage.
2. People in the United States and Canada often go to nutritionists.
3. Many people in the United States and Canada are using traditional treatments instead of modern medicine to treat a variety of health problems.

 **exercise 6** Write a topic sentence for your paragraph.

_____

_____

3. Developing Cohesion and Style

Using Restrictive Relative Clauses

Good writers combine short sentences with relative pronouns to make longer, more natural sentences. The relative pronoun *who* is used for people. The relative pronoun *that* is used for things.

examples: There are many people in the United States and Canada.
They are trying acupuncture. →
There are many people in the United States and Canada *who* are trying acupuncture.

Aspirin is a very common medicine.
Aspirin is used to treat headaches and colds. →
Aspirin is a very common medicine *that* is used to treat headaches and colds.

Notice that *who* and *that* replace the subjects of the second sentences.

 **exercise 1** Combine these sentences with the relative pronoun *who* or *that*.

1. Acupuncture is an ancient treatment. This treatment developed in China.

_____

2. An acupuncturist is a person. This person uses needles to treat diseases.

_____

3. Many people find acupuncture helpful. They experience pain. _____

_____

4. Acupuncturists also use herbs. These herbs help treat the problem.

_____

_____

Chapter Seven • Health   **89**

Chinese acupuncture chart

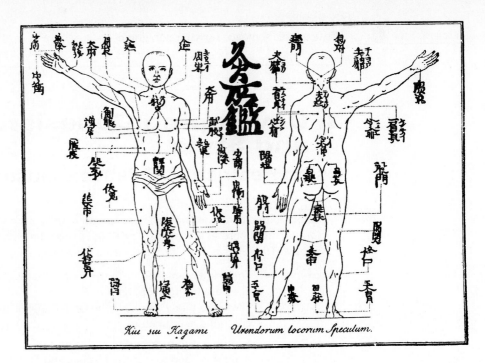

Kiu su Kagami   Urendorum locorum Speculum.

Complete these sentences with relative clauses that begin with *who* or *that*.

1. There are many traditional remedies _____

_____

2. People _____

often use herbs to treat diseases.

3. I knew a woman _____

4. There are many plants _____

_____

Using Transitional Words and Phrases:
in addition, *for example*, and *however*

Transitional words and phrases help unify a paragraph. They can be used to add information, give examples, or give contrasting information. They often come at the beginning of a sentence and are followed by a comma.

• **Adding Information: *in addition***

In addition is similar to *and* and *also*. Use *in addition* when you are adding information after a long sentence or after several sentences.

Herbal remedies, Peru

> example: People used to drink special teas to cure many illnesses. Herbalists made some of these teas from the bark of certain trees. *In addition*, they sometimes made a cream with certain kinds of bark to put on cuts and bruises.

- **Giving Examples: *for example***

  Use *for example* when you want to give specific examples.

  > example: Many people go to psychic healers. *For example*, my cousin went to a psychic healer who cured his high fever with the touch of her hands.

- **Giving Contrasting Information: *however***

  However is similar to *but*, but it often appears in more formal writing. It is used to give contrasting information.

  > example: Some psychic healers can cure many diseases. *However*, others just take people's money and don't help them.

 **exercise 3**   Complete the sentences with *in addition*, *for example*, or *however*.

1. There are many Chinese acupuncturists in Canada. Many of them studied acupuncture in China and then immigrated to Canada. _____ , many Canadian doctors are now giving acupuncture treatments.

2. I often drink herbal teas when I am sick. _____ , if I am very sick, I take modern medicine.

3. Some people in California use many traditional treatments from various parts of the world. _____ , they use remedies and treatments from China.

4. My grandmother often goes to an old lady who gives her strange treatments. _____ , these treatments don't usually help her.

5. I take lemon juice for colds. I put it in a cup of warm water and drink it several times a day. _____ , I take it for sore throats and fevers.

exercise 4 After each sentence write another sentence that begins with *for example*, *in addition*, or *however*. Put commas after the transitional words.

1. I don't use traditional treatments. _____

_____

2. Many herbal teas are good for digestion. _____

_____

3. She went to a nutritionist. _____

_____

4. Psychologists can help you with many problems. _____

_____

5. It's important to have healthful foods. _____

_____

Showing Purpose and Giving Reasons

In Chapter Five, you learned how to use *because* to show reasons.

example: My mother went to an acupuncturist *because* she didn't like to take medicine.

An infinitive (*to* + verb) can also show reason or purpose.

example: I drank herbal tea *to cure* my sore throat.

exercise 5  Read this paragraph and answer the questions that follow.

You don't have to spend a lot of money at a pharmacy to treat a cold because there are many inexpensive old remedies that are just as good as the newer ones. For example, my grandmother always advised us to drink honey and lemon juice in hot water to cure coughs. People who study natural medicine now say that lemon juice is good for colds because it kills germs, and honey contains natural elements that improve health. In addition, my mother used a natural remedy to help me breathe better when I had a cold. She put me in a room full of steam. Doctors still recommend this remedy. Because scientists haven't found any easily available medicine that kills viruses which cause colds, there isn't any cure for the common cold. I therefore think honey, lemon juice, and steam are safer than chemicals with long names I can't pronounce.

1. Underline the reason why lemon juice is good for colds. What word introduces the reason? _____

2. Find a reason that comes at the beginning of a sentence. Circle it.

3. Find two examples of infinitive expressions that show purpose. Draw two lines under them.

4. Writing the First Draft

Now write your paragraph about traditional treatments that people in your culture use. Give reasons and examples and show purpose when you can. Use these expressions:

1. Examples: *for example*
2. Reasons and purposes: *because, to* + verb
3. Additional reasons or examples: *in addition, also*

Give your opinion in the last sentence of your paragraph.

5. Editing Practice
Using Editing Symbols

You learned some editing symbols in Chapter Six, page 81. Here are some more symbols your teacher may use.

sp The spelling is wrong.

vt The tense of the verb is wrong.

ro You wrote a *run-on* sentence. A run-on sentence is an incorrect sentence that should be two sentences:

                                    ro
He ate only junk food and never exercised, in addition he stayed up late nearly every night.

↻ You should move the circled part to where the arrow points.

≡ Capitalize the letter.

ww The word is wrong. Some words are almost synonyms, but each has special uses.

              ww
I like to swim to rest.

exercise 1   Rewrite these sentences correctly.

1. many people in the Philippines drink herb teas. _____
   _____

2. The healer gave (to my friend) a foot massage∨. _____
   _____

3. Three years ago he have a stomach ache. _____
      ^wt^
   _____

4. His leg did not cure. _____
      ^ww^
   _____

5. My friend didn't like to go to doctors, he went to a psychic. _____
                                           ^ro^
   _____

exercise 2   Edit this paragraph twice and rewrite it correctly. The first time, add transitional words and phrases such as *for example*, *however*, and *in addition*. The second time, add commas after transitional words and dependent clauses that begin sentences. Also use commas before conjunctions when you combine two complete sentences.

> Some people can cure themselves of cancer with traditional treatments. I know a woman who cured herself of cancer by fasting. She didn't eat for one month and then she slowly began to eat again. When she completed the fast she had completely cured herself of cancer. I read about a man who cured his cancer using an old Chinese diet. As soon as he started the diet he began to get better. Scientists don't have a modern drug to cure cancer.

Chinese herbal medicines

6. Editing Your Writing

 Edit your paragraph using the following checklist.

Editing Checklist

1. Content
   a. Is the information interesting?
   b. Are there purposes and examples in the paragraph?
2. Organization
   a. Does the topic sentence give the main idea of the paragraph?
   b. Are all the sentences about the topic of the paragraph?
3. Cohesion and Style
   a. Did you use relative clauses correctly?
   b. Did you use transitional words and phrases correctly?
4. Grammar
   a. Did you use correct noun forms?
   b. Did you use correct verb forms?
5. Form
   Are there commas after transitional words and after dependent clauses?

exercise 2 Exchange papers with another student and edit each other's writing. You can use some of the editing symbols you learned in Chapter Five and on page 93 of this chapter.

Herbal Shop

Recognizing Correct Usage of Transitional Phrases

This is a new section that helps you with skills for taking writing tests, including standardized tests such as the TOEFL. Recognizing the correct usage of transitional phrases is often tested in a multiple-choice format. The following exercise will give you practice using this format.

Read the following paragraph and choose the correct transitional phrases from the lists below to use in the numbered spaces.

Jethro Kloss was an herbalist. He treated many Americans who doctors couldn't help. _____ he wrote an important book about
₁
traditional treatments. Mr. Kloss encouraged the use of natural remedies.

_____ he said that a good diet with plenty of fruit and
₂
vegetables was very important. As a treatment for disease, he recommended special cold and hot water baths. He _____ advised
₃
his patients to get a lot of exercise. Because he knew about hundreds of herbs, he was one of the most famous herbalists in the United States.

1. (a) In addition,
   (b) For example,
   (c) However,
   (d) Because

2. (a) For example
   (b) Example,
   (c) For example,
   (d) example

3. (a) however
   (b) in addition
   (c) too
   (d) also

7. Writing the Second Draft

Rewrite your paragraph using neat handwriting and correct form. Then give it to your teacher for comments. When your teacher returns your paragraph, look at his or her comments. Do you understand your teacher's editing symbols? Ask if there are symbols you don't understand.

A STEP beyond

activity 1

Your class can make a short book of traditional treatments throughout the world. Type or write your paragraphs neatly and put them together in a folder or binder. Some students can draw or find pictures for the book. You can pass the book around the class or give it to another English class to read.

activity 2

Write about an illness or health problem you or a family member has or had. Describe the illness. How are/were you treating the problem? Are/were you getting good health care?

activity 3

Write the two headings listed below on the blackboard. Under each heading list the different features of medical care in the United States and in other countries.

MEDICAL CARE IN THE UNITED STATES   MEDICAL CARE IN OTHER COUNTRIES

activity 4

Write for ten minutes about which is better—medical care in the United States or medical care in your home country. Use the features listed in Activity 3 to give reasons for your opinion. Exchange papers with another classmate and discuss your opinions.

Journal Writing

activity 5

Write in your journal for ten minutes about one or more of the following topics.

1. Things to do to stay healthy
2. How I keep my good health/What I do that is bad for my health
3. The oldest person I know

Chapter Seven • Health

WHAT DO YOU THINK?

Comparing and Contrasting Traditional and Modern Medicine

1. In what ways are modern and traditional medicine different?
   What features can you find in both? List them in the chart
   below. Use the features listed here and others you can think
   of. Remember that different people may have different
   opinions about whether something is a feature of modern or
   traditional medicine. Give reasons for your choices.

   • Is expensive/is inexpensive
   • Requires formal training to practice/doesn't require
     formal training to practice
   • Is dangerous/is not dangerous
   • Can be used to treat serious diseases/can't be used to
     treat serious diseases
   • Is natural/is artificial
   • Is controlled by the government/isn't controlled by the
     government
   • Can be used to cheat people/can't be used to cheat
     people

   TRADITIONAL MEDICINE   MODERN MEDICINE

   _____   _____

   _____   _____

   _____   _____

   _____   _____

   _____   _____

   _____   _____

2. Write in your journal or dicuss which you think is better—
   traditional or modern medicine. Use the features in the chart
   to give reasons for your opinion.

CHAPTER eight

Entertainment and the Media

in this chapter

You will write a paragraph about your favorite movie.

STEPS TO writing

1. Exploring Ideas
Describing and Categorizing Movies

exercise 1 Look at the photos from these movies and match them with the movie categories below.

musical   comedy   horror
science fiction   drama   action/thriller

1. *The Chinese Connection*

Category: _____

2. *A Night at the Opera*

Category: _____

3. *Star Wars*

Category: _____

4. *Singing in the Rain*

Category: _____

5. *Like Water for Chocolate*

Category: _____

6. *Frankenstein*

Category: _____

 Discuss these questions in small groups.

1. What kind of movie do you like best?
2. What kind of movie do you like least?
3. What is your favorite movie? Who are the stars of that movie? Who are the main characters? What type of movie is it? When and where does it take place?

Building Vocabulary

 Circle the adjectives that describe your favorite movie.

exciting	realistic	action-packed
funny	sad	well-written,
fascinating	imaginative	well-directed
horrifying	touching	frightening
interesting	entertaining	heart-warming

 Who is your favorite character in the movie? What is he or she like? Circle the adjectives that describe him or her.

crazy	talkative	loyal
funny	brawny	smart
angry	shy	brilliant
evil	talented	magical
fun-loving	ambitious	hard-working
brave	kind	successful

activity **5**   List any other adjectives that describe this character.

      _____   _____   _____

      _____   _____   _____

      _____   _____   _____

      _____   _____   _____

2. Organizing Ideas

Summarizing a Movie Plot

> When you write about your favorite movie, you will include a summary of the plot. A good way to do this is to first write a list of events from the movie and then to choose the most important and interesting events to include in your summary.

exercise **1**   Look at the following list of events from the movie *The Wizard of Oz*. Then write a similar list of events in your favorite movie. Don't worry about grammar or form. If there are any words you don't know in English, write them in your native language. You can look them up in a dictionary later if you choose to include the event in your summary.

EVENTS FROM *THE WIZARD OF OZ*

1. Dorothy tries to run away from home.
2. A tornado carries her far away to a magical place.
3. She meets the Munchkins and tells them she wants to go home.
4. The Munchkins tell her to follow a yellow brick road to the Emerald City, where a wizard will help her.
5. On her journey, she meets a scarecrow. He joins her to ask the wizard for a brain.
6. They meet a tin woodsman who goes with them to ask for a heart.
7. They meet a cowardly lion and take him along so he can ask the wizard for courage.
8. They finally reach the Emerald City and see the wizard.
9. The wizard tells them they must find the bad witch and bring him her broom before he will help them.
10. The witch locks Dorothy up in her castle.
11. Her friends try to save her.
12. The witch sets the scarecrow on fire.
13. Dorothy throws water on the scarecrow, but misses him.
14. The water hits the bad witch and she melts.
15. They take the broom to the wizard.

Scene from the movie *The Wizard of Oz*

16. The wizard shows the scarecrow, the tin woodsman, and the lion that they already have what they are looking for.
17. Dorothy clicks her heels together three times and says, "There's no place like home."
18. She wakes up in her own bed.
19. She discovers that her adventure was only a dream, but that she learned an important lesson.

Including Important Information in a Summary

A good movie summary should be more than a list of events. It also tells the *problem* and events leading to a *solution*. In addition, a good movie summary includes only important events—the ones that relate the problem and the solution. Finally, a good movie summary shows the relationship between important events.

 **exercise 2** Read the following two summaries of *The Wizard of Oz*. Which is the better summary of the movie? Why? Think about these questions:

- What is the problem in The Wizard of Oz? What is the solution?
- Which paragraph includes the important events that show the problem and the solution?
- Which paragraph relates events better?

Summary 1

The Wizard of Oz is the story of Dorothy, a girl from Kansas. A tornado carries her to Munchkinland. She meets the Munchkins and a good witch named Glynda. The Munchkins are small people who sing and dance. They tell her to follow a yellow brick road to find a wizard. They sing a song about the yellow brick road. She meets a scarecrow who wants a brain, a tin woodsman who wants a heart, and a lion who wants courage. They go with her to find the wizard. A bad witch locks her up in a castle, but her friends try to save her. The witch sets the scarecrow on fire. When Dorothy throws water on the scarecrow, she misses him, but the water hits the bad witch and she melts. She finds the wizard in the Emerald City and gives him the witch's broom. The wizard uses a machine to scare people, but he is really an ordinary man. She clicks her heels three times, then wakes up and realizes it was only a dream.

Summary 2

The Wizard of Oz is the story of a young girl named Dorothy, who tries to run away from home. A tornado carries Dorothy off to a magical land. In this magical place, she meets many strange and wonderful characters, but Dorothy wants to get back home again. A scarecrow who wants a brain, a tin woodsman who wants a real heart, and a cowardly lion who wants courage, all travel with her to the Emerald City to ask a great wizard for help. A bad witch tries to keep them from finding the wizard, while a good witch helps them on their journey. With the help of the wizard, who is really an ordinary man, and the good witch, they all learn important things about themselves, and they get what they are looking for. When Dorothy learns that home is the best place on earth, she is able to return. She realizes that her adventure was only a dream, but one with an important lesson.

 **exercise 3**   Look at the list of events you wrote from your favorite movie. Which events are the most important? Are there any events that you can combine to show their relationship?

 **exercise 4**   The paragraph that follows includes all the information in the list below. Read the paragraph, find all the information listed, and write it on the lines.

1. The type of movie _____

2. Where the movie takes place _____

3. When the movie takes place _____

4. The problem _____

5. The result _____

6. The main characters _____

7. Why you like the movie _____

E. T.: THE EXTRA-TERRESTRIAL: A HEARTWARMING ADVENTURE

One of my favorite movies is *E. T.: The Extra-Terrestrial*, a touching science fiction story about the friendship of a young boy and E. T., a creature from outer space. It takes place in the 1980s in a small American town. When E. T.'s spaceship leaves without him, he meets Elliot, a boy who becomes his friend. E. T. likes Elliot, but he is very homesick, so Elliot decides to help him contact his friends. This is not easy because some scientists are searching for E. T. in order to study him. Elliot and E. T. escape from the scientists by bicycle. They go to the woods to meet the spaceship that will take E. T. home, and in a beautiful scene, they say good-bye. I found everything I like best in movies in *E. T.* The characters are wonderful, and it has great suspense, a magical story, and an ending that moved me to tears.

 **exercise 5**   Look at your list of events from your favorite movie. Make a list of any other information you would like to add.

Writing a Title

> If you give your paragraph an interesting title, people will want to read it. Titles of movies are underlined (or put in italics in printed material). All the important words in a title (of a movie, book, etc.) begin with a capital letter. Small words such as *and, in, a, the, to, at,* or *with* do not begin with a capital letter unless they are the first words in the title.
>
> *examples:*   *The Story of Qui Ju*
> *Dona Flora and Her Two Husbands*

Chapter Eight • Entertainment and the Media

Punctuate the titles in parentheses and capitalize words that need capital letters.

1. You should see (the seven samurai), a classic Japanese film.
2. The Brazilian actress Sonia Braga was in (kiss of the spider woman).
3. The Marx brothers appeared in (a day at the races) and (the big store).
4. The most famous American movie is probably (gone with the wind), the story of Southern families during the Civil War.
5. I saw (the sorrow and the pity) yesterday.

Look at the following titles. Which movies would you like to read about? Why?

1. *The Godfather:* My Favorite Movie
2. *E. T.:* An Unforgettable Experience
3. *The Wizard of Oz:* A Good Movie

Write a title for your paragraph.

3. Developing Cohesion and Style
Using Adjectives

> One way to make a movie summary interesting is to add adjectives that describe characters and events

Look back at the list of adjectives on page 101 that describe movies in the section Building Vocabulary. Find appropriate adjectives and write them above the carets (^) in the following sentences.

1. *Star Wars* is a˄ science-fiction movie.

2. *Dracula* is a˄ horror movie about a vampire.

3. *The Godfather* is a˄ drama about organized crime in the United States.

4. *Schindler's List* is a˄ drama about a German who saved the lives of many Jews.

Write a similar sentence about your favorite movie.

_____

_____

 **exercise 3** Make a list on the board of some of your favorite movie characters. Look back at the list of adjectives on page 101 that describe characters in the Building Vocabulary section. In small groups, write phrases describing those characters using the adjectives on the list or other adjectives.

> example: *E. T.—a magical visitor from another planet*
> *Rambo—a brawny ex-soldier*

Using Appositives

> You can combine sentences using appositives. An appositive is a phrase that modifies a noun and follows it directly. It is separated from the rest of the sentence by commas.
>
> *examples:* Han Solo is one of the heroes of *Star Wars*. He is a brave but self-centered pilot. →
> Han Solo, *a brave but self-centered pilot*, is one of the heroes of Star Wars.
>
> *E. T.* and *Jurassic Park* were directed by Steven Spielberg. He is one of America's most popular filmmakers. →
> *E. T.* and *Jurassic Park* were directed by Steven Spielberg, *one of America's most popular filmmakers*.

 **exercise 4** Can you find any appositives in the paragraph about *E. T.: The Extra-Terrestrial*? Underline them.

 **exercise 5** Combine the following sentences by using appositives. Remember to use commas.

1. *Gone with the Wind* takes place in the South of the United States. It is a film about the U.S. Civil War. _____

   _____

2. In *Jurassic Park*, the dinosaurs seem totally real. It is a comic and hair-raising thriller. _____

   _____

3. The beautiful and thought-provoking *Guelwaar* was written and directed by Ousmane Sembene. He is Africa's foremost filmmaker. _____

   _____

4. Tom Hanks starred in *Philadelphia*. It is the story of a young lawyer who has AIDS. _____

   _____

Using the Historical Present Tense

> Look back at the paragraph about *E. T.: The Extra-Terrestrial*. What tense is it in? You can use the present tense to talk about movies that describe events in the past. This is the "historical present."

exercise **6**   Look at the following paragraph and complete it with the correct forms of the verbs in parentheses. Use the historical present.

It's a Wonderful Life _____ (be) a heartwarming drama. In this
₁
movie, James Stewart _____ (play) an ordinary family man who
₂
_____ (live) in a small American town. When he is about to lose his
₃
business because of a serious mistake, Stewart _____ (become)
₄
very depressed. He _____ (try) to jump off a bridge, but an angel
₅
_____ (show) him how important he _____ (be) to his
₆ ₇
friends, family, and the community. He then _____ (decide) not to
₈
kill himself.

WHAT DO YOU THINK?

Choosing Movies

How do you choose the movies you see? What do your movie choices say about you as a person? To find out, try the following activity.

1. Here are some possible reasons for choosing a movie. Put a check (✓) next to the reasons that are important to you in choosing a movie. If you have other reasons, write them in the blanks.

   _____ the director   _____ the setting (where

   _____ the actors   and when story takes place)

   _____ the story   _____ special effects

   _____ music   other: _____

   _____

2. **Think about the last five movies you chose to see. They can be movies you saw in a theater, rented on video, or watched on TV. Write the names of these movies in the chart below. (Don't list movies you saw because someone else chose them!) Next to each movie, write your three most important reasons for choosing it. One movie is done for you as an example.**

	reasons for choosing it		
name of movie	most important	very important	important
The Remains of the Day	story	actors	director
1.			
2.			
3.			
4.			
5.			

3. **When you finish, look at your list of movies and reasons. Do you see any similarities or patterns in your choices? For example, do you have a favorite actor or director? Do you like movies about different times in history? Do you usually choose movies for the same reason(s)?**

4. **Work with a partner. Exchange charts and look at your choices of movies. How are your choices and reasons similar or different? Did you see any of your partner's movies? Why or why not?**

5. **Write in your journal for ten minutes about what you learned from this activity. Do you plan to see different kinds of movies in the future?**

4. Writing the First Draft

Write the paragraph about your favorite movie. Use important events and information, and combine sentences to show the relationship between events. Also include adjectives and appositives to describe the movie and characters. Use the title you wrote. You can write the paragraph in the historical present tense.

5. Editing Practice

Using Two or More Adjectives

> • Sometimes you may want to use more than one adjective. You can separate two or more adjectives with a comma.
>
> *examples:* E. T. is a friendly, lovable creature from outer space.
>
> In the movie *Rocky*, the main character is a handsome, determined boxer.
>
> • When there are two contrasting adjectives, you can separate them with *but*.
>
> *example:* In *Star Wars*, Han Solo is a brave *but* self-centered pilot.

 Look at these sentences. Put a comma between the two adjectives.

1. *Gandhi* is the story of a wise kind man who leads India to freedom.
2. In *It's a Wonderful Life*, James Stewart plays a hard-working ordinary man.
3. *The 400 Blows* tells the story of a lonely unhappy boy.
4. *Women on the Verge of a Nervous Breakdown* contains many colorful comic characters.

 Put the word *but* in the appropriate places in the sentences.

1. *Gandhi* is about a gentle powerful leader.
2. *Frankenstein* is the story of a destructive tragic monster.
3. *The Godfather* is about an evil loyal man.
4. The lead characters in *Thelma and Louise* are vulnerable brave.

 Edit the paragraph on page 111 twice and rewrite it correctly. The first time you edit, take out any unnecessary details. The second time, change the verbs to the historical present, correct punctuation, and make any other changes you think are necessary.

Star Trek II is a science fiction film. *Star Trek* was first a television series, and this is the second *Star Trek* movie. In this movie, Khan, an evil but clever leader stole information about a secret government experiment. Leonard Nimoy played Mr. Spock. The crew of the spaceship *Enterprise* had to catch Khan before he could use the information. Captain Kirk and his crew succeeded as usual, but in the end, the captain lost a good friend. Which one of the crew died? See the movie and find out it's definitely a good film to watch. I liked this movie a lot. Maybe you will too.

6. Editing Your Writing

 Edit your paragraph using the following checklist.

Editing Checklist

1. Content
   a. Is the title interesting?
   b. Would others want to see the movie because of your summary?
   c. Did you present the problem and the events leading to the solution?
   d. Does your summary include the type of movie, when and where the movie takes place, and the main characters?
2. Organization
   a. Is all the information in the paragraph important?
   b. Does the topic sentence give a general idea of what kind of movie you're writing about?
3. Cohesion and Style
   a. Did you combine sentences to show the relationship between events?
   b. Did you use appositives correctly?
   c. Did you use adjectives to describe the characters and the movie?
   d. Did you use the historical present tense?
4. Grammar
   a. Are the present-tense verbs correct?
   b. Are the count and non-count nouns correct?
   c. Did you combine sentences correctly?
5. Form
   a. Did you underline the title of the movie?
   b. Did you use commas with appositives and adjectives correctly?
   c. Did you punctuate combined sentences correctly?

Exchange papers with another student and edit each other's paragraphs.

7. Writing the Second Draft

> After you and another student edit your paragraph, rewrite it using neat handwriting and correct form. Then give it to your teacher for comments.

focus on testing

Summarizing

Summarizing can be a useful test-taking skill. You have been practicing this skill throughout the chapter, and making a summary of a movie is no different than making a summary of a book or other series of events. You must choose the important events, give the background, and relate the problem and the events leading to a solution. The following exercise will give you more practice in writing summaries.

With a partner, choose a book, movie, TV program, or historical or current event that you are both familiar with. Write a summary of it. Then exchange summaries and compare them. How are they the same or different? Did your partner include information that you did not?

A STEP beyond

activity **1**

Read three of your classmates' movie summaries. Discuss which movies you would like to see and why. If you have seen any of the movies, tell whether you agree with your classmates' summaries.

Journal Writing

activity **2**

Write in your journal for ten minutes about one or more of the following topics:

1. Violence in movies
2. Why I like (or don't like) movies
3. My favorite book
4. A current event

CHAPTER nine

Social Life

You will write about a classmate's life in the past year.

in this chapter

STEPS TO **writing**

1. Exploring Ideas
Interviewing Someone

exercise 1 Look at these pictures of Tony, an international student studying English. Then describe Tony. What has be been doing during the past year? How has he been feeling? Use the information in the pictures and add other information. Write as many sentences as you can in ten minutes.

English 208

present perfect
continuous

TOM'S TRUCKING

6:05

 Discuss the kind of information you wrote in your sentences. Did you write about any of the following topics? What did you say about each topic?

- Family life
- Social life
- Work
- Accomplishments
- Unusual or special events

 Write questions about the preceding topics. Think of other questions you could ask a student in your class. Your teacher will list them on the board.

 Use the questions from Exercise 3 to interview a student about his or her life in the past year. Take notes on the information your partner gives you.

Building Vocabulary

 The chart below has examples of vocabulary you can use to talk about life events. What other new words can you add from your discussions and interview? In small groups, discuss the meaning of any words you do not understand.

NOUNS	VERBS	ADJECTIVES	OTHER
accomplishment	accomplish	exhausted	_____
hobby	attend	fascinating	_____
recreation	_____	_____	_____
_____	_____	_____	_____
_____	_____	_____	_____
_____	_____	_____	_____
_____	_____	_____	_____
_____	_____	_____	_____
_____	_____	_____	_____
_____	_____	_____	_____
_____	_____	_____	_____

2. Organizing Ideas

You are going to write a paragraph about a student in your class for a class newsletter. The paragraph will say what the student has been doing for the past year.

Writing Topic Sentences

Topic sentences about what someone has been doing for the past year are often in the present perfect tense (*have/has* + past participle) or the present perfect continuous tense (*have/has* + *been* + verb + *ing*).

examples: June Nomura *has lived* in Texas since April.

Ben Rodriguez *has been working* in a hospital.

Which of these sentences are good general topic sentences for a paragraph about Tony's life during the past year? Circle the numbers of those sentences. Which sentence do you think is the most interesting? Put a check by it.

1. Tony Prado has had a busy life this year.
2. Tony Prado has been married since June.
3. This year Tony Prado has had so much to do he has felt like a juggler.
4. Tony Prado has learned a lot of English this year.
5. During the past year Tony Prado has gotten married, worked at two jobs, played soccer, and studied English.
6. During the past year Tony Prado has had a full but happy life.

Write a topic sentence for your paragraph. Use the present perfect or the present perfect continuous tense.

_____

_____

Organizing Information in a Paragraph

> There are two ways to organize your paragraph:
>
> 1. You can begin with more important activities such as work, and you can end with less important activities such as hobbies or interesting events.
> 2. You can begin with difficult activities and end with more enjoyable activities.

 Look at the following notes about Tony's life. Work in small groups and arrange them in order. Use one of the two types of organization above.

> goes to English classes—has no time to study
> works in uncle's factory—makes him tired
> got married in June—a lot of responsibility
> goes riding with his wife
> works evenings in a beauty salon
> plays soccer with friends

 Look at your notes from your interview and arrange them in the order you think you are going to write about. Discuss the order with your partner.

Writing a Concluding Sentence

> The final sentence in this kind of paragraph can summarize the paragraph or indicate some future action.

 Look at these examples of possible final sentences.

1. In November, Tony's wife is going to have a baby, and then he will have another thing to juggle in his busy schedule.
2. With her new English skills, Sonia is hoping to get a better job.
3. Parvin says that it's a full-time job to take care of her kids, but she can't wait till they are in school and she can get a job that pays money.
4. Satoshi is going to return to Japan and use his English in his engineering work.

 Write a final sentence you could use in your paragraph.

_____

_____

3. Developing Cohesion and Style
Selecting the Correct Tense

> It's important for each sentence in a paragraph about someone's life to be in the correct tense. You can use the following chart to check your verb tenses.

verb tenses	notes and examples
Simple Present	A repeated or habitual action in the present. _example:_ Mina **studies** English in Austin, Texas.
Present Continuous	An action or situation that is _in progress_ in the present. _example:_ Mina is **studying** and **working** this quarter.
Future	An action or state that will occur in the future. _example:_ Mina **will be** in Texas for at least two years.
Past	A completed action or state. _example:_ Mina **came to** Austin three months ago.
Present Perfect	An action or, more usually, a state (with verbs like _be, have, feel, know_) that began in the past and continues in the present. Often appears with _for_ and _since_ + time expression. _example:_ Mina **has known** her friend Salima since 1986; she **has known** her friend Sally for one month.
Present Perfect Continuous	An action that began in the past and continues in the present; often appears with _for_ and _since_ + time expression. _example:_ Mina **has been working** part time in the school cafeteria since she arrived (for three months).

Complete this paragraph with the correct tenses of the verbs in parentheses. Remember that you can use the present perfect or the present perfect continuous to introduce a subject and then use the present tense to talk about it further.

This year Tony _____ (have) so much to do he
1
_____ (feel) like a juggler. He _____ (get)
2   3
married in June, He and his wife are very happy together but now

he _____ (have) a lot more responsibility. He _____
4   5
(work) in his uncle's factory since April. It _____ (be) hard
6
work, because he _____ (have) to load trucks and he
7
_____ (get) very tired. In addition, he _____ (work)
8   9
a few evenings a week as a hairdresser because he _____ (need)
10
to save money. He also _____ (take) English classes at a
11
community college near his home. He _____ (enjoy) the class,
12
but he _____ (be) so busy he _____ (not have) much
13   14
time to study. Tony's life _____ (not be) all work, however.
15
In fact, he still _____ (find) time to enjoy a few sports. He
16
_____ (play) soccer with some friends every Sunday. In
17
addition, he and his wife often _____ (go) bike riding together.
18
But she is pregnant now and _____ (have) a baby in four
19
months. Then Tony _____ (have) another thing to juggle in
20
his busy schedule.

Write five sentences from your interview notes. Underline each verb, then check to see if you've used the correct form.

Using Transitional Words and Phrases

However, in addition, also

The expressions *however, in addition,* and *also* help unify the sentences in a paragraph.

exercise 3   Find the expressions *however*, *in addition*, and *also* in the paragraph about Tony on page 119 and underline them. Then answer these questions.

1. Which two expressions do you use when you give additional information?

   _____

2. Which expression do you use when you give contrasting information?

   _____

3. In the paragraph about Tony, is this expression in item 2 at the beginning or end of the sentence? _____

4. Can the expression be in another position? _____

In fact vs. **however**

In Chapter 7, you learned to use *however* to give contrasting information. You can use *in fact* to give facts that show that the sentence before is true. Use a comma to separate *in fact* from the rest of the sentence.

example: Tony has been very busy. *In fact*, he's been working at two jobs.

   Add *in fact* or *however* to these sentences. Remember to use commas where necessary.

1. Tony has been working very hard. He works from 8:00 in the morning until 9:00 at night. _____

   _____

2. Tony has been working very hard. He still finds time to play soccer every week. _____

   _____

3. Raúl has been doing well, and he likes his English class a lot. He's been studying so much that he isn't sleeping well. _____

   _____

4. Raúl has been doing well in his English class. He went from level 2 to level 4 last month. _____

   _____

Look at your notes and write some pairs of sentences for your paragraph. Begin the second sentence of each pair with a transitional phrase: *however, in fact, also,* or *in addition.*

_____

_____

_____

_____

_____

_____

_____

_____

_____

_____

Stating Results with *so . . . that*

You can combine sentences giving reasons and results by using *so . . . that.*

Reason   **Result**

Tony has been busy.   +   He has felt like a juggler.
Tony has been so busy that he has felt like a juggler.

Combine these sentences using *so . . . that.*

1. Jane has been busy. She hasn't had much time to study. _____

_____

2. Reiko was happy. She cried. _____

_____

3. Chi Wang has been working hard. He falls asleep in class. _____

_____

4. Nick has been having much fun. He is seldom homesick. _____

_____

5. Sonia's daughter has been sick. She had to take her to the hospital.

_____

 **exercise 7** Can you write any sentences with *so . . . that* for your paragraph? Write them here.

_____

_____

_____

_____

_____

_____

_____

_____

_____

_____

_____

_____

4. Writing the First Draft

Now write your paragraph about a classmate. Use your topic sentence and notes. Also use transitional expressions to unify your paragraph.

5. Editing Practice
Using Long Forms in Formal Writing

When English speakers write formally, they don't use as many contractions as when they speak—instead, they use long forms. Here are some examples of long forms and their contractions:

he has → he's   he has not → he hasn't
they have → they've   they have not → they haven't
it is → it's   it is not → it's not, it isn't

Write these sentences without contractions.

1. He's been playing in a band. _____

_____

2. They haven't moved yet. _____

_____

3. They're not having problems with Canadian customs. _____

_____

_____

4. Recently she's been planning a party. _____

_____

_____

5. It's difficult work. _____

_____

6. She's been getting dates from a computer dating service. _____

_____

Spelling Present and Past Participles Correctly

Write the *-ing* form and the past participle of these words. The first one is done as an example. (For rules for adding *-ing*, see Appendix One, page 174.)

		-ing FORM	PAST PARTICIPLE
1.	work	working	worked
2.	begin	_____	_____
3.	study	_____	_____
4.	make	_____	_____
5.	find	_____	_____
6.	swim	_____	_____
7.	go	_____	_____
8.	travel	_____	_____
9.	come	_____	_____
10.	have	_____	_____

Using Correct Capitalization

In your paragraph, remember to capitalize time words correctly. (See Appendix Two, page 176, for detailed rules.)

- Capitalize months and days of the week.

  examples: July   September   Monday   September

- Don't capitalize seasons.

  examples: summer   fall   winter   spring

- Capitalize names of schools and businesses.

  examples: Lincoln Community College   Lucia's Bakery
  University of Montreal   Interspace, Inc.

- Don't capitalize kinds of schools, businesses, or jobs.

  examples: a bakery   a baker
  an export company   an accountant
  a community college   a musician

- Don't capitalize school subjects except languages.

  examples: business math   French
  biology   English

 *exercise* 3   Write these sentences with correct capitalization.

1. Pablo has been studying computer science and english at northwestern college since january. _____

   _____

2. Anna works as a dietician at randolph college. _____

   _____

3. In september Van got a job as a mail clerk at a bank. _____

   _____

4. Tessa has been studying fashion design every tuesday and thursday evening. _____

   _____

5. Irena has been working with the jones plumbing company since the fall.

   _____

   _____

Edit this paragraph twice and rewrite it correctly. The first time, see if the ideas are well organized. Do you need to rearrange any sentences? The second time, correct any problems with verb tenses and form. Make any other changes you think are necessary.

Marta Duarte has have a very interesting year. Last June she graduated from a tourism development course in Mexico. She received a scholarship to study English and has been attending classes here at the University of Ottawa since September. marta is twenty-five years old. She's also been traveling in Canada and the United States. She love dance and goes dancing at least two nights a week. She visits hotels to study the different management systems and has learned a lot. In fact, she says that one day in a hotel is better than ten days in a classroom. However, Marta hasn't spend all her time in Canada at work. She also find time to develop a close friendship with the manager of a big hotel here in Ottawa. She is hoping to get to know him better.

6. Editing Your Writing

Edit your paragraph using the following checklist.

> **Editing Checklist**
>
> 1. Content
>   a. Is the information interesting?
>   b. Is all the information in the paragraph important?
> 2. Organization
>   a. Does the topic sentence give the main idea of the paragraph?
>   b. Are the sentences well organized?
>   c. Does the paragraph have a good concluding sentence?
> 3. Cohesion and Style
>   a. Did you use transitional expressions correctly?
>   b. Did you use *so . . . that* correctly?
> 4. Grammar
>   Did you use correct verb forms?
> 5. Form
>   a. Did you use commas correctly?
>   b. Did you spell the verb forms correctly?
>   c. Did you use correct capitalization?

exercise **2**   Exchange papers with a classmate and discuss the changes you made.

7. Writing the Second Draft

> Write the second draft of your paragraph using neat handwriting and correct form. Then give it to your teacher for comments.

A STEP beyond

 *activity* **1**   As a class, collect all the paragraphs to make a class newsletter.

 *activity* **2**   Recopy your paragraph without the name of the classmate you interviewed. Give your paragraph to another of your classmates. Can he or she guess who you wrote about?

 *activity* **3**   Write a paragraph about what you have been doing in the past year.

activity **4**   Write a paragraph about your plans for the future.

activity **5**   Write about what you and a group of people (your English class for example) have been doing.

Journal Writing

 *activity* **6**   Write in your journal for ten minutes three days in a row. Reread your writing. Does anything surprise you?

WHAT DO YOU THINK?

Evaluating a Day in Your Life

How do you spend your time on a typical day? Do you spend time on things you really want to do? To find out, try the following activity.

1. Draw a large circle on a piece of paper with a pencil. Think of this circle as one day in your life.
2. Divide your circle into four quarters using dotted lines. (Each quarter = 6 hours of the day.)
3. Look at the questions below. Divide your circle to show about how many hours you usually spend on these items. Draw lines and label the parts of your circle as in the example. (*Important:* There is no "right" or "wrong" way to do this. Everyone's life is different!)

How many hours do you spend
- Sleeping?
- In school?
- On homework?
- Working (if you have a job)?
- Traveling (to and from school, work, etc.)?
- With friends?
- With family (if you are living with family)?
- Alone (doing activities of your choice)?
- On other activities (use your own examples)?

4. When you finish, look at your drawing. Are you happy with the way you are spending your time?
5. Draw another circle. This time, divide the circle to show how you *would like* to spend the day.
6. If you like, share your circle drawings with another student. Do you want to change the way you spend your time? If so, in what way(s)?
7. Write in your journal for ten minutes about what you learned from this activity.

Managing Your Time

One of the greatest problems in taking an essay exam is learning to use your time wisely. For example, you should take time to plan, but if you take too much time, you won't have enough time to write. Therefore, when you take an essay exam, you should divide your time this way:

Thinking about the topic	10%
Planning and making notes	10%
Writing	70%
Revising and editing	10%

CHAPTER ten

Customs, Celebrations, and Holidays

Mask festival in Central America

in this chapter

You will write a paragraph about holidays in your home country.

STEPS TO **writing**

1. Exploring Ideas
Describing Holidays

exercise 1 Look at the photographs and discuss them. What do you know about the holidays the people in the photos are celebrating?

Christmas

Carnival, Brazil

Chinese New Year

Rocket festival, Thailand

exercise 2   What are the most important holidays in your home country or culture? When do people celebrate these holidays? How do they celebrate them? Complete the following chart.

HOLIDAY	TIME OF YEAR	ACTIVITIES	DESCRIPTION OF ACTIVITIES
_____	_____	_____	_____
_____	_____	_____	_____
_____	_____	_____	_____
_____	_____	_____	_____
_____	_____	_____	_____
_____	_____	_____	_____
_____	_____	_____	_____
_____	_____	_____	_____
_____	_____	_____	_____

exercise 3   Look at your list of holidays. How could you divide them into groups? Try dividing them by seasons first (winter holidays, summer holidays). Then suggest other ways to group them (by activity, purpose, etc.).

_____

_____

_____

_____

_____

_____

_____

_____

_____

_____

_____

_____

_____

_____

_____

_____

Building Vocabulary

The chart below has examples of vocabulary you can use to talk about holidays. What other words did you use to describe holidays? Add your words to the list. Discuss any words you do not understand

NOUNS	VERBS	ADJECTIVES	OTHER
celebration	celebrate	traditional	_____
commemoration	commemorate	joyous	_____
parade	_____	_____	_____
fireworks	_____	_____	_____
tradition	_____	_____	_____
_____	_____	_____	_____
_____	_____	_____	_____
_____	_____	_____	_____

2. Organizing Ideas
Categorizing and Making an Outline

Some people organize their ideas in outline form. First they write notes about their topic. Then they divide the notes into categories. Finally, they write an outline.

Here is an example of the notes that an American student made about holidays in her country.

Christmas	Independence Day	Memorial Day	Easter
New Year's	Presidents' Day	Labor Day	Passover
Thanksgiving	Valentine's Day	Halloween	Hanukkah

She decided to divide the holidays into three categories.

1. Political holidays
2. Religious holidays
3. Traditional holidays

Before the student began to write her paragraph, she made an outline:

    I. Holidays in the United States

        A. Political holidays

            1. Independence Day

            2. Presidents' Day

            3. Memorial Day

            4. Labor Day

B. Traditional holidays
1. Thanksgiving
2. New Year's
3. Halloween
4. Valentine's Day
C. Religious holidays
1. Christian holidays
a. Christmas
b. Easter
2. Jewish holidays
a. Passover
b. Hanukkah

Does your country have any political holidays? Traditional holidays? Religious ones? Make an outline like the one the student from the United States made.

Ordering Information According to Importance

When you expand an outline, you usually put the items in order of importance.

Here is part of an outline a student made about holidays in the United States. It shows the order of importance of traditional holidays. Can you explain why she chose this order? Notice that 1. a., 2. a., and 3. a. all have the same type of information.

B. Traditional holidays
1. Thanksgiving
a. Third Thursday in November
b. People feel thankful for the good things in their lives
c. Families eat turkey and other traditional foods
2. New Year's Day
a. January 1
b. People celebrate the New Year
3. Halloween
a. October 31
b. Children dress in costumes
c. People go to costume parties
d. Children collect candy

This student decided to write about political holidays. She added more information to her outline, but some information is missing. Read her outline, and then read the paragraph after it on page 135. Fill in the student's outline with the missing information.

I. Holidays in the United States

   A. Political holidays

      1. Independence Day

         a. Fourth of July

         b. _____

         c. Picnics, barbecues

         d. Fireworks

      2. _____

         a. Last weekend in May

         b. Commemorate the American soldiers who died in all wars

         c. Parades

         d. Put flags and flowers on graves

         e. _____

      3. Labor Day

         a. _____

         b. Honor American workers

         c. Parades

         d. Picnics, beach

         e. _____

      4. _____

         a. _____

         b. Honor George Washington's and Abraham Lincoln's birthdays.

HOLIDAYS IN THE UNITED STATES

There are three types of holidays in the United States: political holidays, traditional holidays, and religious holidays. There are more political holidays than any other type. The most important political holiday is Independence Day, the Fourth of July. On this day we celebrate our independence from Great

5　Britain. Most people spend the day with their family and friends. Picnics and barbecues are very popular. In addition, almost every city and town has a fireworks display at night. Another very important political holiday is Memorial Day, which falls on the last weekend in May. On this holiday we commemorate all the soldiers who died for our country. Many towns and cities have parades,

10　and some people go to cemeteries and put flowers or flags on the soldiers' graves. A third important political holiday is Labor Day, which we celebrate on the first Monday in September. This is the day when we honor the workers of the United States. People watch parades, go on picnics, or go to the beach. For students, Labor Day is a bittersweet holiday, because when it is over they

15　must begin school again. Besides these three political holidays, we also celebrate Presidents' Day on the third Monday in February. On this day we commemorate the birthdays of George Washington and Abraham Lincoln.

Fourth of July parade

 Make an outline for the type of holiday you are going to write about.

3. Developing Cohesion and Style

Listing Information with *in addition to, besides, another,* and *the first, second, third, last*

> You can use these transitional words to add information: *in addition to, besides, another,* and *the first, second, third, last.*
>
> examples: *In addition to* watching parades and going on picnics, some Americans also go to the beach on Labor Day.
>
> *Besides* Thanksgiving and New Year's Day, there are other traditional holidays in the United States such as Halloween and Valentine's Day.
>
> The *first* holiday of the year is New Year's Day.

 Look at the paragraph about holidays in the United States on page 135. Underline the transitional words that are used for adding information.

 The following paragraph contains no transitional words. Complete it with the appropriate transitions. More than one answer may be correct.

> Salvadorans celebrate several political holidays each year. The most important one is Independence Day on September 15. On this day, people parade in the streets, sing songs, and recite poems. _____
> important political holiday is Labor Day. Labor Day is the first day in May.
> _____ Labor Day and Independence Day, Salvadorans also
> celebrate the birthday of José Matias Delgado, the "father of the country."
> _____ these holidays, there are other minor holidays such as
> el *Dia de la Raza.*

Unifying a Paragraph with Pronouns and Pronominal Expressions

> You can use pronouns to refer to things you have already mentioned so that you don't have to repeat the same words again and again.

 **exercise 3**   Here is a list of the pronouns and pronominal expressions in the paragraph about holidays in the United States on page 135. Tell what each one refers to.

1. on this day (line 4) _____

2. on this holiday (line 8) _____

3. this is the day (line 12) _____

4. it (line 14) _____

5. they (line 14) _____

6. these three political holidays (line 15) _____

 **exercise 4**   The paragraph that follows needs more pronouns. Edit it and substitute pronouns or pronominal expressions for *some* of the nouns. Remember that too many pronouns are as bad as too few.

Americans celebrate several traditional holidays. One traditional holiday Americans celebrate is New Year's. Many people often go to parties and drink champagne on New Year's Eve. In fact, New Year's is the first holiday of the year. In addition, on New Year's Eve, Americans sometimes wear silly hats and blow horns. At midnight, Americans kiss the people near them and wish everyone a Happy New Year at New Year's Eve parties.

Using Quantifiers

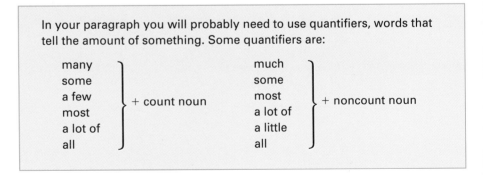

In your paragraph you will probably need to use quantifiers, words that tell the amount of something. Some quantifiers are:

many			much		
some			some		
a few	} + count noun		most	} + noncount noun	
most			a lot of		
a lot of			a little		
all			all		

 **exercise 5**   How many quantifiers can you find in the paragraph about holidays in the United States? Underline them.

Using Nonrestrictive Relative Clauses

- In Chapter Seven you learned about restrictive relative clauses with *who* and *that*. A restrictive relative clause tells you which person or thing the writer is referring to.

  examples: Ramadan is the Moslem holiday *that lasts a month.*
  Moslems *who observe Ramadan* fast (do not eat) from sunrise to sunset during this month.

- A nonrestrictive relative clause gives additional information. In nonrestrictive clauses, use *which* instead of *that*. Use commas to separate a nonrestrictive clause from the rest of the sentence.

  examples: Thanksgiving, *which falls in November*, is a time for families.

  Another traditional holiday is Halloween, *which is mainly for children.*

- The information in a nonrestrictive relative clause is not necessary. You can omit a nonrestrictive relative clause, but you cannot omit a restrictive relative clause.

  examples: Thanksgiving, *which falls in November,* is a time for families to get together. (nonrestrictive)

  Notice that you can omit the clause *which falls in November: Thanksgiving is a time for families to get together.*

  Christmas is the holiday *that I like best.* (restrictive)

  Notice that if you omit the clause *that I like best,* the sentence seems incomplete: *Christmas is the holiday.*

 **exercise 6**   Combine these sentences with *which* and a nonrestrictive relative clause. Insert a clause at the ∧ mark.

1. Easter ∧ is a happy holiday. Easter comes in the springtime. _____

   _____

   _____

2. The Fourth of July ∧ is a time for big parades and fireworks. The Fourth of July is Independence Day. _____

   _____

   _____

3. Martin Luther King Day ∧ comes in January. Martin Luther King Day is

our newest holiday. _____

_____

_____

4. Halloween ⌃ is a favorite children's holiday. Halloween is an ancient

British tradition. _____

_____

_____

5. On New Year's Day ⌃ there is a famous parade in Pasadena, California.

New Year's Day is the first holiday of the year. _____

_____

_____

exercise **7** Write three sentences using nonrestrictive relative clauses about the holiday in
your outline. Use correct punctuation.

_____

_____

_____

WHAT DO YOU THINK?

Examining the Meaning of Holidays

Holiday celebrations are so common all over the world that
most people do not question why we have holidays. In small
groups discuss the following.

1. **What are some different
purposes of holidays in
your home country?**

2. **Are some holidays more
special or important to
some people (or groups
of people) in your country
than to others? Why?**

3. **Are there any holidays in
your country that used to be
important but aren't now? Why?**

4. **In your country, are there
any controversial holidays—
holidays that not everyone
agrees should be celebrated?
If so, why do people disagree?**

4. Writing the First Draft

Write your paragraph about holidays in your culture. Use your outline and the sentences you wrote using nonrestrictive relative clauses.

5. Editing Practice
Punctuating Nonrestrictive Relative Clauses

* Use commas to separate a nonrestrictive clause from the rest of the sentence. If the clause comes in the middle of the sentence, use two commas.

  examples: Valentine's Day, which falls on February 14, is a holiday for lovers.

* If the clause comes at the end of the sentence, use only one comma.

  examples: Memorial Day is in May, which is almost the beginning of the summer in the United States.

 Add commas where necessary in these sentences.

1. Songkran which is the Thai New Year is on April 13.

2. Eid-e-Ghorbon is a religious holiday in Iran which is a Muslim country.

3. Christmas which is an important holiday in Christian countries is usually a happy time.

4. Bastille Day which is on July 14 is a very important holiday in France.

 Edit the paragraph on page 141 and rewrite it correctly. The first time, check to see if the order of ideas is correct. (See the outline on page 133 if you need help.) The second time, check to see if the writer has used quantifiers correctly. Make any other changes you think are necessary.

There are four important traditional holidays in the United States. Another important traditional holiday is New Year's. On New Year's Eve, most people go to parties. At twelve o'clock, everyone shouts "Happy New Year!" and they wish their friends good luck. New Year's parties usually last a long time. Some people don't go home until morning. The most important of these holidays is Thanksgiving, which we celebrate on the third Thursday in November. This is a family holiday. Most of people spend the day with their relatives. They feel thankful for the good things in their lives. The most important tradition on this day is Thanksgiving dinner. At a traditional Thanksgiving dinner, the most people eat turkey with stuffing, cranberry sauce, and pumpkin pie. The third traditional holiday, Halloween, is mainly for children. On this holiday, people dress as witches, ghosts, or other such things. Much children go from house to house and say "Trick or treat." If the people at the house do not give them candy, the children will play a trick on them; but, this hardly ever happens. A most give them candy or fruit. Another holiday is Valentine's Day, which is in February. On this day, people give each other cards, flowers, or candy.

Children in
Halloween costumes

6. Editing Your Writing

 Edit your paragraph using the following checklist.

> ### Editing Checklist
>
> 1. Content
>   a. Is the information interesting?
>   b. Is there enough information?
> 2. Organization
>   a. Did you list the holidays from most important to least important?
>   b. Did you give the same type of information about each holiday?
> 3. Cohesion and Style
>   a. Did you use expressions such as *in addition to, besides, another, the first (second,* etc.)?
>   b. Did you use quantifiers correctly?
>   c. Did you use pronouns and pronominal expressions appropriately?
>   d. Did you use relative clauses correctly?

 Exchange papers with a classmate and discuss the changes you made.

7. Writing the Second Draft

> Write the second draft of your paragraph using neat handwriting and correct form. Then give it to your teacher for comments.

A STEP beyond

 Bring in pictures to illustrate different holidays that your class celebrates. Write captions and put the pictures on a bulletin board.

 With other students from your country, make a book about holidays in your country. Use pictures and writing to explain the holidays. Share your book with your classmates.

  **activity 3** Write a paragraph about your favorite holiday.

 **activity 4** Interview a classmate about her or his favorite holiday. In a paragraph, explain why it is her or his favorite.

Journal Writing

activity 5 Write in your journal about how you feel about spending holidays away from home and what you miss most.

Traditional holiday food at a Korean first birthday.

Organizing Your Ideas

When taking an essay exam, it is important to organize your ideas before you write. This will make your paragraph flow more smoothly. The following steps can help you organize your writing.

1. Read the topic carefully.
2. Make notes on the different points you want to write about.
3. Organize your notes. Group similar points together. Number the points (or groups of points) from the most important to the least important.
4. Check to make sure that all your points relate to the topic; delete any points that don't.
5. Write your paragraph using your organized notes.

To practice this skill, organize some notes on the following topics:

Being an International Student Is a Challenge
Why Good Nutrition Is Important
Why I Like Living in the City (or Country)

Science and Technology

in this chapter

You will write a message to a computer newsgroup about control of electronic communication.

STEPS TO **writing**

1. Exploring Ideas
Discussing Computer Networks and Newsgroups

A computer network connects different computers so people and computers can share information, send each other e-mail (electronic mail) and participate in electronic discussions called newsgroups, bulletin boards, or conferences. The following article discusses these points.

The Internet Infohighway

*I*n recent years, there has been a revolution in communication that has connected people all over the world. You can now sit at your desk, make a local telephone call from your
5 computer, and connect to a network which will allow you to explore information in computers from Acapulco to Zhenjiang.

You can find out soccer scores for your hometown team, shop for the latest com-
10 puter equipment, discuss your favorite movie star with an electronic friend thousands of miles away, read and post articles on the latest international crisis, or play chess with a team of international players.
15 Using a kind of software called "gophers," you can search for information in computer databases all over the world. In thousands of computer newsgroups, you can read and "upload" (or send) messages on almost any
20 subject—some of which you wouldn't want your children to see. With some computers, you can even play music and "download" (or receive) photographs.

The network with the most information
25 is the Internet (or "Net"). The Net started as a way for scientists and computer experts to communicate and share information. Universities, research groups, and governments paid for it, and only people with advanced
30 computer knowledge could use it. Now almost anyone can access the Internet, and they can send or receive almost any kind of information. This freedom of access can be good or bad, and there are many unanswered
35 questions about it, such as:

- Should governments, or any other group, try to control the Internet?
- Should there be advertising? Who should control it?
40 - Should the Internet carry *any* kind of communication? What about censoring criminal activity, racist messages, or sex discussions or pictures?
- Should people be allowed to "flame"
45 (verbally attack) *anyone* or *any* subject?

These questions of freedom versus control will never be answered to everyone's satisfaction, and they will probably be the
50 subject of interesting newsgroup discussions for a long time.

exercise 1   Look at the four questions near the end of the article. Discuss them in small groups with other students.

Building Vocabulary

exercise 2   This chart has examples of terms commonly used in computer networking. Add other words you used in your discussion to the list. Then choose the correct terms from the list to complete sentences 1 to 6 that follow the chart.

NOUNS	VERBS	OTHER
network	network	_____
gopher	censor	_____
e-mail	download	_____
censorship	upload	_____
infohighway	flame	_____
electronic	access	_____
newsgroup	_____	_____
access	_____	_____
_____	_____	_____
_____	_____	_____

1. When you want to send a message you have already written to a newsgroup, you can _____ it to the group in only a few seconds.

2. An electronic _____ is a group of computers connected together to communicate and share information.

3. By using a _____ , you can search for information on any subject in a computer network.

4. When you connect to the Internet, you have _____ to computers around the world.

5. You can _____ a message from a newsgroup to save it on your computer.

6. People on the Internet do not agree on how to _____ illegal activity.

2. Organizing Ideas
Organizing Computer Newsgroup Messages

You are going to write a message to a computer newsgroup on the topic of censorship. In your message, you will give your opinion about one of the four questions in the article you just read.

Messages to newsgroups are generally organized like other writing, with a few minor differences. Here are a few special rules for organizing newsgroup messages. Many of these "rules" have developed informally and are referred to as "netiquette." (*Netiquette* is a combination of the words *network* and *etiquette;* the word *etiquette* means "*a set of rules for good behavior.*")

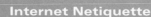

Internet Netiquette

- Because so many messages are sent to computer newsgroups, keep your message short.
- Keep to the topic of the newsgroup. You may be flamed if you don't!
- Keep your message simple and informal. Newsgroups are for ordinary people. Don't try to use big words and difficult sentences.
- If you are responding to another message, quote a few lines from the message so people who didn't read it know what you are talking about. Each line of a quote on the Internet begins with a forward bracket (>).
- Give your main idea in a few sentences so people can quote a few lines from your message when they reply to it.
- People on the Internet express their opinions strongly, and you can find some very strong personal attacks on the Net. Express your opinion strongly, but don't call people names or attack them personally when you disagree with them.
- Don't only criticize other messages—offer positive suggestions.
- Don't type in all capital letters. On computer networks, this means you are angry and are SHOUTING.

 **exercise 1**   Read the two messages on page 149 from the newsgroup on censorship. Each one contains information that is not on the subject of computer network censorship. Find that information and cross it out. (Note that at the beginning of the article, the computer automatically includes the topic, time and date of writing, computer "address" of the writer, and the name of the newsgroup between asterisks ** **.)

```
**Topic: Ban Advertising on the Internet**
**Written 10:10 am Jan 5, 1995 by lmbewe@dlu.edu**
***Advertising ruins our cities, our highways, our magazines, and
our TV. Every night I have to throw away dozens of pieces of junk
mail I receive that advertise products I don't want. The U.S. mail
system has gotten so bad that I don't receive mail I need, only
stupid advertisements. Someone must do something about it! Can you
imagine what would happen if people could send junk mail to
thousands of Internet users just by hitting a few keys on their
computer? The Internet would be finished! Can't there be at least
one place where human beings can communicate without some people
trying to make money off us?
Lionel Mbewe
lmbewe@dlu.edu
```

The second message is a response to Lionel. Note that when some Net users sign
their name, they may also include their regular address and/or one of their favorite
quotations.

```
**Written 8:32pm Jan 7, 1995 by freebie@freepr.mrfs.qu.ca**
>Can't there be at least one place where human beings can
>communicate without some people trying to make money off us?
It would be nice, but let's be real: it would be impossible to
keep advertising out of the Internet. In fact, it is already here,
in special newsgroups that share information about different
products. One of the freedoms that we have is the freedom to make
money, as long as the making of money does not break some other
law. We have to make realistic rules to control advertising on the
Net, not to ban it completely. Why don't all the people involved
in this question--companies who want to advertise, ordinary people
against advertising, the groups that provide access to the Net,
and experienced users--get together on-line and seriously work
toward setting controls on advertising? Right now it's just talk,
talk, and more talk!
So many people who send messages to the Internet are scientists
and university researchers who live far away from the real lives
of most of us who need to make money. They don't need to advertise
on the Internet--they have good safe jobs. University professors
should be required to spend time outside in the real world before
they go into the classroom and try to tell us ordinary people the
way it is.
Cindy McPherson, People's Free Press, 7592 rue Berri, Montreal,
Quebec, H2J 2R6, Canada freebie@freepr.mrfs.on.ca
''None can love freedom heartily, but good men -- the rest love
not freedom, but license.'' - John Milton
```

Chapter Eleven • Science and Technology

 In groups, discuss what you crossed out on page 149 and why it doesn't belong.

 Cindy quoted the lines she thought gave the main idea of Lionel's message. What lines would you quote as the main idea of Cindy's message? What positive suggestion did Cindy give?

Choose one of the four questions in the article on page 146. Write two or three sentences that give your opinion about the question. Offer positive suggestions if possible and make sure you are writing only about that topic. If you want to respond to one of the messages above, mark the sentences that you will quote to give the main idea of the message you are responding to.

Supporting Your Opinion

> While your newsgroup message should be short, it should include support for your opinion. That is, you need to give examples or reasons that illustrate your point of view or prove your argument.

 In her reply to Lionel, Cindy wrote that it would be impossible to keep advertising out of the Internet. She gave one supporting example and one supporting reason. What are they?.

Supporting example: _____

_____

Supporting reason: _____

_____

exercise 6 Read the newsgroup message below. The writer first quotes another message and then gives his opinion. Find the writer's opinion and underline it.

```
**Written 11:25 am Mar 17, 1995 by m janovic@comp. usc. ca.us**
>Words cannot hurt anyone. Any censorship, no matter how well-
>meaning, will in the end be used to prevent people from speaking
>their mind. The Internet, now a wild and wonderful place, will
>become just another piece of media controlled by people with
>money.

I don't understand how anybody can argue for total freedom from
censorship on the Internet. I can only think that they don't have
children. I have two daughters, aged 10 and 14. They see me using
the Internet and are anxious to learn how. And I'm anxious for
them to get involved. However, I don't let them have access when
I'm not around. There are controls on sex and violence in other
media: why not on the Internet?

Mike Janovic m janovic@comp. usc.ca.us
```

exercise 7

In small groups, discuss what examples or reasons Mike could give to support his opinion by answering the following questions. Write your answers on the lines below.

1. Why would a parent be anxious for her or his children to get involved in the Internet? _____

_____

_____

2. Why wouldn't a parent want his or her children to have access to the Internet when he or she is not around? _____

_____

Look at the sentences you wrote in Exercise 4 giving your opinion about one of the four questions in the article on page 146. Write each sentence again. Under each sentence, give reasons and examples supporting your opinion.

Writing Newsgroup Topic Lines

Computer newsgroup messages don't include titles. Instead, the topic is written after the word **Topic:**, which appears on the computer screen. This topic is just like a title: It should give the main idea of your message and make people want to read it. The topic is included in the index of messages, which people use to decide which messages to read, so it is important. When writing your topic, follow the same rules of capitalization as you do for titles.

Write a topic for the message from Mike Janovic above.

Topic: _____

Write a topic for the message you are going to write.

Topic: _____

_____

3. Developing Cohesion and Style

Unifying Your Writing with Synonyms and Pronouns

One way of unifying your writing is to refer to the same word or topic several times. However, a paragraph doesn't flow smoothly if you often repeat the same word in phrases that are near each other. To refer to a word or topic in a nearby phrase, you should use:

* pronouns such as *it, they, this* and *these,* or
* synonyms (words with the same or similar meaning), often used with *this* or *these*

If you haven't used a word in a few sentences, then you can repeat it.

 Look at the third paragraph in the article on page 146 about the Internet. Find and underline the pronoun "it" and the synonym "the Net" where these terms are used to refer to the Internet. Note that the word "Internet" is repeated a few times also.

Look at this list of words with similar meanings. Insert the appropriate words in the sentences that follow.

computer (used as adj)—electronic

censor—control (v)

access (v)—connect to

criminal (used as adj.) — illegal

The Internet is a huge computer network. People connected to the Net can participate in _____ discussions called bulletin boards. Because
₁
so many people can now _____ these bulletin boards, the
₂
question of who should control information on the Internet is an important topic for discussion. For example, should the government try to _____ the Internet for racist messages or _____
₃   ₄
activity?

Language for Giving Opinions and Suggestions

> There are phrases you can use to give polite opinions; there are also suggestions and phrases you should avoid if you want to be polite. Use *should, need to, it would be better if,* or *why don't / doesn't* instead of *must.*
>
> examples: The Internet *should* censor messages for racist language.
>
>   *Why doesn't* the Internet censor messages for racist language?
>
>   The Internet *needs to* censor messages for racist language.
>
>   *It would be better if* the Internet censored messages for racist language.

 Find the language Cindy and Lionel used on page 149 to give opinions and suggest ways they can make their messages more polite.

 Look at the opinions and suggestions you wrote earlier in the chapter. Have you expressed them politely?

4. Writing the First Draft

Using the opinions and supporting reasons and examples you have written, write your newsgroup message. Make sure you state your main idea somewhere in your message and support your opinion with reasons and/or examples. First write a topic line, your message (quoting another message if you like), and then your name and electronic address. If you don't have an electronic address, write your first initial and last name, the "@" symbol, the initials of your school, a period, and then "edu," as in the following example:

`blelieu@und.edu`

WHAT DO YOU THINK?

Considering Personal Privacy in the Workplace

In the United States, there are laws to protect people's personal privacy. For example, personal letters and telephone conversations are considered private. It is illegal to read someone else's mail or to listen in on someone's telephone line without that person's permission. There are also new laws to protect users of electronic communications such as e-mail. However, these law are not always clear.

Today many companies tell their employees that they can use their computers and electronic networks—including e-mail — for company work only; they cannot use them for any personal (non-company) purpose. Furthermore, companies say they have the right to read the content of employee's electronic messages without their permission. Employees who are found using computers or e-mail for nonbusiness purposes may lose their jobs.

What do you think of such a business policy? Do you think a company has the right to read its employees' e-mailwithout asking their permission? Should an employee lose his or her job over using e-mail for a nonbusiness purpose, such as sending an e-mail message to a friend? How do people's privacy rights in your country compare with those in the United States?

5. Editing Practice
Spelling and Grammar in Computer Messages

Luckily for non-native speakers of English, one of the netiquette rules is not to flame people for grammar or spelling mistakes. Of course, you should use correct grammar and spelling so your message is clear and easy to read. (If someone does flame you, you might write back asking how well they would communicate in your native language!) If you are writing on a computer, use a computer spell-check program.

exercise

Edit this reply to Mike Janovic, who wanted censorship in the Internet. First omit any personal attacks or lines that aren't on the topic. Then add support to the opinion expressed and/or give a positive suggestion. Finally, use pronouns and/or synonyms in place of the word "Internet" and correct spelling and grammar. (Note that since you can't underline on the Internet, writers use asterisks ** instead.)

Response 1 of 1

```
>I don't understand how anybody can argue for total freedom from
>censorship on the Internet. . . . There are controls on sex and
>violence in other media: why not on the Internet? That's just the
point: the Internet is *not* like all other media. It is selfish
peabrains like Mr. Janovic who one day ruin the Internet. The In-
ternet not for childs, the Internet for adults. If peple want a
Sesame Street Internet, they should make there own Internet and
not ruining our Internet. Childs must to be controled. Parents let
them run wild in the street. They taking drugs and killing peple.
```

6. Editing Your Writing

 Edit your message using the following checklist.

Editing Checklist

1. Content
   a. Does the message express your opinion strongly without personal attacks?
   b. Have you given reasons and examples to support your opinions?
2. Organization
   a. Are all your sentences on the topic of the newsgroup?
   b. Does your message contain a sentence or two that gives the main idea of your message?
   c. Does your topic line give the main idea of your message and make people want to read it?
3. Cohesion and Style
   a. Does your message use pronouns and synonyms to unify your writing?
   b. Have you used polite phrases to give opinions and suggestions?
4. Grammar
   a. Are your verbs correct?
   b. Have you used correct grammatical forms to give opinions and suggestions?
5. Form
   a. Have you avoided writing in all capitals?
   b. Have you capitalized the important words in your topic line correctly?
   c. Have you put front brackets before lines quoting other messages?
   d. Have you written a signature under your message with your name and electronic address?

 Give your message to another student to check.

7. Writing the Second Draft

Rewrite your message using neat handwriting and correct form. Then give it to your teacher for comments.

A STEP beyond

activity 1   If you can connect to a computer network (many universities have Internet connections) that has newsgroups on computer censorship and control, you can actually send your messages. Find a newsgroup topic, send your message, and see what replies you receive. If you don't have access to a computer bulletin board, you can use a regular bulletin board. Post your messages on the board, and students from your class or another class can read the messages and respond to them.

activity 2   Look at this list of newsgroup "addresses" and descriptions. When you participate in newsgroups, you can look at an index of messages that people post and choose which ones to read. You can download the most interesting ones onto your computer to read later, and you can upload messages of your own. Which newsgroups would you be interested in reading? Which ones would you like to write about? What would you write? Would you like to visit or start a newsgroup on another topic? What would the subject be?

`alt.shy.support`	A discussion by and about shy people.
`biz.ad.internet`	A discussion about advertising on the Internet.
`tesl.l`	Questions and answers about teaching English as a second language.
`comp.support.com`	Questions and answers about problems with communications software.
`rec.soccer.intl`	A discussion about international soccer/football.
`soc.immigra`	A discussion about immigration in America.
`talk.flame.congress`	"Flames" or attacks on the U.S. congress.
`alt.best.of.internet`	A place where people post their favorite messages.

activity 3   If anyone in the class has access to newsgroups and can print out messages, print out some of your favorites. Read or duplicate them so your classmates can respond to them.

Chapter Eleven • Science and Technology

157

Journal Writing

The following activity is called a free association exercise. Choose one of the topics below. As quickly as possible, write down all the words you associate with that topic. Don't censor or omit any word you think of, no matter how silly or unrelated to the subject it seems. (Write the words in your native language if you don't know them in English). Then write your opinion of the topic using some of the words from your free-association practice.

1. Computers
2. Advertising
3. The English language
4. Writing
5. Your home

focus on testing

Making an Outline of Supporting Examples and Reasons

On essay tests that require you to express your opinion about a topic, it's very important to include supporting examples and reasons. An outline can help you organize your ideas quickly. Write your opinion(s), leaving space for supporting examples and reasons. Then ask the question "why?" to think of supporting examples and reasons and note them on your outline. You can then be sure that you have supported each opinion with reasons and examples.

CHAPTER twelve

You, The Consumer

You will write a letter of complaint about something you bought that you are dissatisfied with.

STEPS TO **writing**

1. Exploring Ideas
Discussing Consumer Problems and Complaints

 Look at the following pictures, which show people who have just bought something that they are not happy with. What's wrong in each picture?

 Discuss these questions in small groups.

1. Have you ever bought something from a store and been disappointed with it? What was the item? What was wrong with it?
2. What did you do? Did you keep the item? Did you take it back? If you took it back, what happened?

Building Vocabulary

 This chart has examples of vocabulary commonly used in talking about consumer problems and complaints. Add other words you used in your discussion to the list. Discuss any words you do not understand.

NOUNS	VERBS	ADJECTIVES	OTHER
refund	refund	defective	_____
receipt	exchange	dissatisfied	_____
guarantee	return	guaranteed	_____
warranty	complain	_____	_____
complaint department	purchase	_____	_____
manager	_____	_____	_____
_____	_____	_____	_____
_____	_____	_____	_____

2. Organizing Ideas
Writing an Effective Letter of Complaint

A well-written letter of complaint should:

1. Be addressed to a person who can do something about the problem.
2. Be polite.
3. State the problem clearly and simply.
4. Give definite details that explain *who* did *what, when, where,* and *why.*
5. Include receipts, order numbers, prices, and other important details if available.
6. Suggest a solution.

**exercise 1** Jaime Flores bought a kitchen appliance from a mail order catalog. Read his letter of complaint. Where does he needs to add details?

Dear Sir,

The other day I ordered an electric frying pan from your catalog. When it arrived, it didn't work. Please refund my money.

Sincerely,

Jaime Flores

Jaime Flores

**exercise 2** Marie Wolpert bought a suitcase at a large department store. She is unhappy with it and would like to return it. Here are notes for a letter that she is writing to the department manager. Read them and draw a line through any unnecessary details.

1. Skyway suitcase
2. 30″ × 45″
3. light blue
4. purchased June 17
5. paid cash
6. reduced from $50 to $42
7. handle broke on trip to Buffalo
8. handle broke first time used
9. called the store
10. spoke with the manager of luggage department on July 15
11. manager said no refunds or exchanges on sale items
12. manager's name Simon Grey
13. would like to exchange suitcase

 **exercise 3**   Think of something you bought that you were dissatisfied with. Make a list of the important details. (If you can't remember all the details, you can write what you think might have happened.)

_____

_____

_____

_____

_____

_____

_____

_____

_____

_____

exercise 4   Exchange lists with another student in your class. Can you understand the situation? Has he or she included all the important information? Has he or she included any unnecessary details?

focus on testing

Evaluating Supporting Details

When judging essay tests, teachers often look for arguments with appropriate and effective supporting details. Essays should include important details to support an argument and not include unnecessary details, just like a letter of complaint.

Look at the list of details you just wrote. How effective do you think they will be in supporting the argument you are making? Are there details you could add or change to make the person you are writing to more likely to respond to your request? Since you are probably writing about an actual event, you may not want to add or change the details in your letter. However, knowing what kind of details are important to an argument and what kind aren't will help you when you take essay tests. You will find exercises at the end of this chapter to help you and your classmates evaluate the effectiveness of supporting details.

3. Developing Cohesion and Style

Using Past Participles as Adjectives

> The past participle of a verb can also function as an adjective. For example, the past participle *broken* functions as part of the present perfect tense in the following sentence:
>
> Oh no! I have *broken* the bowl!
>
> However, in this sentence, *broken* functions as an adjective:
>
> When the bowl arrived, it was *broken*.

exercise  Look at these verbs and write their past participles. Then use the past participles as adjectives in a sentence.

example: stain _stained_

The blouse is stained with tomato juice.

1. smash _____

_____

2. open _____

_____

3. destroy _____

_____

4. tear _____

_____

5. fade _____

_____

6. dissatisfy _____

_____

7. rip _____

_____

8. scratch _____

_____

Look at the notes you made in Exercise 3 on page 162 about something you bought that you were dissatisfied with. Write five sentences about your complaint using past participles as adjectives.

Using Formal Language

A business letter should be formal and polite. People generally use more formal vocabulary in business letters than in letters to friends. To make a business letter polite, you shouldn't be too direct. Generally, the fewer words you use at the beginning of a complaint or request, the more direct and less polite it is. To make a request more polite, add polite words or phrases to the beginning of the sentence:

Less Polite: Refund my money.

                                              Please refund my money.

                              Would (Could) you please refund my money?

More Polite: I would appreciate it if you would refund my money.

Look at the following letter of complaint. Rewrite it to make it more formal and more polite.

Dear Sir,

    Last week I bought a set of six glasses in your store. You sent them to my home. When I got the package, four of the glasses were broken. I want a refund for all six glasses. Send it to me soon.

Sincerely,

Kate Collins

Kate Collins

_____

_____

_____

_____

_____

_____

_____

_____

_____

_____

4. Writing the First Draft

Write the first draft of your letter of complaint. Use your notes and the sentences you wrote using past participles and adjectives. Remember to include all important details without adding unnecessary information. Also add polite expressions to any requests you make.

5. Editing Practice
Following the Format of a Business Letter

Look at the business letter on page 166. It shows one correct format for a business letter. (There are several correct formats.) Then do the exercise on page 167.

{
15 South Cedar Street
Boston, Massachusetts 02214
January 11, 19XX

Manager
Sales Department
Universal Publishing Company
1523 Castleton Boulevard
New York, New York 10027
} **Inside Address**

Dear Sir: **Salutation**

On December 15, 19XX I ordered one copy of <u>The United States in Pictures</u> by Jerome Massanti. I included a check for the full price of the book, $18.97 plus $2.00 for shipping and handling charges. On December 27 of last year, I received a letter from your order department that said that the book would not be available until May of this year. The letter also said that if I wanted a refund, I could have it. On January 2, I wrote and asked them to refund my $20.97. It is now four weeks later, and I still have not received my refund.

Would you please look into this matter for me? I have often ordered books from your company and would like to continue doing business with you.

} **Body**

Closing   Very truly yours,

Signature   Simon La Grande

Simon La Grande

A business letter should contain all the following elements:

Heading   The heading gives the writer's address and the date. It should be in the upper right-hand corner of the first page, an inch or more from the top. The address should include:

- number and street or post office box number
- city, state or province, postal code
- country (if the letter is sent out of the country)

Inside Address   The inside address contains the name and the address of the person or company you are writing to. It is usually on the left, two spaces below the date. If you know the name and title of the person, you should include them. For example:

David Pearson, Manager
Sales Department

Margaret McGraw, Customer Relations

Salutation   The salutation or greeting should be two spaces below the inside address. The most common salutations are:

Dear Sir or Madam: Dear Ms. Kaplan:
Dear Mr. Fraser: Dear Mrs. Foster:

Body   The body of the letter begins two spaces below the salutation. You should indent the paragraphs. There should be a margin of at least one inch on both sides of the paper, at the top, and at the bottom. If your letter is very short, you should make your margins larger.

Closing and Signature   The closing is two spaces below the last line of the body. A comma follows it. Capitalize only the first word. Some common ways to close formal letters are:

Very truly yours,   Sincerely,
Yours truly,   Sincerely yours,

Sign the letter about one-half inch below the closing. Then type or print your name under your signature.

Put the information on the top of page 168 into the correct place in the letter form below it. Add commas where necessary.

Customer Service Department, Sullivan Office Furniture
Company, 1432 Bradley Boulevard, Muskegon, Michigan 49441
July 12, 19XX
Dear Sir:
157 John Street, New York, New York 10038

Yours sincerely

Jane Fulton

Jane Fulton
Office Manager

XXXXXXXXXXXXXXXXXXXXXXXXXXXXXXXXXXXXXXXXXX
XXXXXXXXXXXXXXXXXXXXXXXXXXXXXXXXXXXXXXXXXX

XXXXXXXXXXXXXXXXXXXXXXXXXXXXXXXXXXXXXXXXXX

XXXXXXXXXXXXXXXXXXXXXXXXXXXXXXXXXXXXXXXXXX

XXXXXXXXXXXXXXXXXXXXXXXXXXXXXXXXXXXXXXXXXX
XXXXXXXXXXXXXXXXXXXXXXXXXXXXXXXXXXXXXXXXXX

Edit this letter twice and rewrite it correctly. The first time, check to see if the writer has used correct business letter form. Then check to see if the writer included all the necessary details, if he should take out some of the details, and if he has used polite, formal language. Make any other changes you think are necessary.

February 24, 19XX

125 South Street
Brattleboro
Vermont 05301

David Drew
Manager Repair Dept.
Empire Typewriter
Company
309 Fourth St.
Pipe Creek, Texas 78063

dear manager
last month I sent my CD player to you for repairs because it wasn't working correctly. I got it for my birthday. You repair department promise to send to me in two weeks. I still haven't gotten it back. I need my CD player now. You had better tell them to repair it and send it to me quickly.

David Wright

6. Editing Your Writing

 Edit your letter using the following checklist.

> ### Editing Checklist
>
> 1. Content
>   Did you explain the problem clearly?
> 2. Organization
>   a. Did you include all the necessary details?
>   b. Did you include any unnecessary details?
> 3. Cohesion and Style
>   a. Did you use formal language?
>   b. Did you use polite language?
> 4. Grammar
>   a. Did you use correct verb forms?
>   b. Did you use past participles as adjectives correctly?
> 5. Form
>   Did you use the correct business letter format, with a date, inside address, salutation, and closing?

 Exchange letters with another student. Discuss the letters. Are there any other changes you should make?

7. Writing the Second Draft

> Rewrite your letter neatly using good handwriting and correct form. Then give it to your teacher for comments.

A STEP beyond

 Exchange letters with another student. Pretend you are the person who received the letter and decide what you will do about the complaint. Either write a reply to the letter or pretend to call the person who wrote the letter on the phone and discuss your decision.

 Write a formal letter complaining about a problem at your school. It might be the courses the school offers, the cafeteria food, the lack of parking spaces, or anything else. Before you write your letter, find out the correct name and title of the person your letter should go to. For example, you might write to the cafeteria manager about a problem with the food. Share your letter with your classmates. If you like, send any letters you feel describe important problems.

 Does your community or school newspaper have a complaint column? Bring in one of the columns if you can find one. In small groups, read a complaint to your classmates and discuss what they think should be done. Then read what the columnist wrote and see how similar it is to what your classmates decided.

Journal Writing

 In your journal, make two columns with these headings at the top:

WHAT I LIKE ABOUT MY LIFE NOW   **WHAT I DON'T LIKE ABOUT MY LIFE NOW**

Quickly make a list of all the things you like and don't like. Then write an informal "complaint" about one of the things you don't like and what you think you can do about it.

activity **5** Write in your journal about the most important thing(s) you have learned about writing in English since you started this course.

WHAT DO YOU THINK?

Analyzing Information Supporting a Complaint

In small groups, read a few of your classmates' letters of complaint. Analyze the information your classmates provided in support of their complaints. For example, consider

- The time period between the purchase and problem
- The claims of advertisements for the product
- Supporting documents such as receipts and names of people

Is the information about the complaint clear and simple? Does the writer suggest a solution? Is the writer polite?

Imagine that your group works for the company or store receiving the complaint letters. What are you going to do about each complaint? Why?

Appendixes

Spelling Rules for Adding Endings

Endings That Begin with Vowels (-ed, -ing, -er, -est)

1. For words ending in a silent *e*, drop the *e* and add the ending.

   like → lik**ed**   make → mak**ing**   safe → saf**er**   fine → fin**est**

2. For one-syllable words ending in a single vowel and a single consonant, double the final consonant.

   ba**t** → bat**ted**   ru**n** → run**ning**   fa**t** → fat**ter**   ho**t** → hot**test**

3. Don't double the final consonant when the word has two final consonants or two vowels before a final consonant.

   pic**k** → pick**ed**   sin**g** → sing**ing**   clea**n** → clean**er**   coo**l** → cool**est**

4. For words of two or more syllables that end in a single vowel and a single consonant, double the final consonant if the word is accented on the final syllable.

   refér → refer**red**   begín → begin**ning**

5. For words of two or more syllables that end in a single vowel and a single consonant, make no change if the word isn't accented on the final syllable.

   trável → travel**ed**   fócus → focus**ed**

6. For words ending in a consonant and *y*, change the *y* to *i* and add the ending unless the ending begins with *i*.

   stud**y** → stud**ied**   dirt**y** → dirt**ier**   sunn**y** → sunn**iest**
   stud**y** → stud**ying**   hurr**y** → hurr**ying**

7. For words ending in a vowel and *y*, make no change before adding the ending.

   pla**y** → play**ed**   sta**y** → stay**ing**

Endings That Begin with Consonants (-ly, -ment)

1. For words ending in a silent *e*, make no change when adding endings that begin with consonants.

   fine → fine**ly**   state → state**ment**

2. For words ending in a consonant and *y*, change the *y* to *i* before adding the ending.

hap**py** → happ**ily**   mer**ry** → merr**iment**

Adding a Final *s* to Nouns and Verbs

1. Generally, add the *s* without making changes.

sit → sit**s**   dance → dance**s**   play → play**s**   book → book**s**

2. If a word ends in a consonant and *y*, change the *y* to *i* and add *es*.

mar**ry** → marr**ies**   stu**dy** → stud**ies**   cher**ry** → cherr**ies**

3. If a word ends in *ch, s, sh, x,* or *z,* add *es*.

chur**ch** → church**es**   ca**sh** → cash**es**   fi**zz** → fizz**es**
bo**ss** → boss**es**   mi**x** → mix**es**

4. For words ending in *o*, sometimes add *es* and sometimes add *s*.

tomat**o** → tomato**es**   potat**o** → potato**es**
pian**o** → pianos   radi**o** → radios

5. For words ending in *f* or *fe*, generally drop the *f* or *fe* and add *ves*.

kni**fe** → kni**ves**   wi**fe** → wi**ves**   li**fe** → li**ves**   loa**f** → loa**ves**
Exceptions: sa**fe** → sa**fes**   pu**ff** → puff**s**   roo**f** → roof**s**

APPENDIX **two**

Capitalization Rules

First Words

1. Capitalize the first word of every sentence.

They live in Rome.   **W**ho is it?

2. Capitalize the first word of a quotation.

He said, "**M**y name is Paul."   Jenny asked, "**W**hen is the party?"

Personal Names

1. Capitalize the names of people including initials and titles of address.

Mrs. **J**ones   **M**ohandas **G**andhi   **J**ohn **F**. **K**ennedy

2. Capitalize family words if they appear alone or followed by a name.

   Let's go, **Dad**.   Where's **Grandma**?   She's at **Aunt Lucy's**.

3. Don't capitalize family words with a possessive pronoun or article.

   my **uncle**   her **mother**   our **grandparents**   an **aunt**

4. Capitalize the pronoun *I*.

   I have a book.   She's bigger than **I** am.

5. Capitalize names of God.

   God   **Allah**   **Jesus Christ**

6. Capitalize the names of nationalities, races, peoples, and religions.

   Japanese   **Arab**   **Asian**   **Chicano**   **Muslim**

7. Generally, don't capitalize occupations.

   I am a **secretary**.   She wants to be a **lawyer**.

Place Names

1. Capitalize the names of countries, states, provinces, and cities.

   Mexico   **New York**   **Ontario**   **Tokyo**

2. Capitalize the names of oceans, lakes, rivers, islands, and mountains.

   the **Atlantic Ocean**   **Lake Como**   the **Amazon**
   Belle Isle   **Mt. Everest**

3. Capitalize the names of geographical areas.

   the **South**   the **East Coast**   **Asia**   **Antarctica**

4. Don't capitalize directions if they aren't names of geographical areas.

   He lives **east** of Toronto.   They traveled **southwest**.

5. Capitalize names of schools, parks, buildings, and streets.

   the **University of Georgia**   **Central Park**   the **Sears Building**   **Oxford Road**

Time Words

1. Capitalize names of days and months.

   Monday   **Friday**   **January**   **March**

2. Capitalize names of holidays and historical events.

   Christmas   **New Year's Day**   **Independence Day**   **World War II**

3. Don't capitalize names of seasons.

   spring   **summer**   **fall**   **winter**

Titles

1. Capitalize the first word and all important words of titles of books, magazines, newspapers, and articles.

   Interactions   *Newsweek*
   The New York Times   "**R**ock **M**usic **T**oday"

2. Capitalize the first word and all important words of names of movies, plays, radio programs, and television programs.

   The African Queen   *The Tempest*   "**N**ews **R**oundup"   "**F**ame"

3. Don't capitalize articles (*a, an, the*), conjunctions (*but, and, or*), and short prepositions (*of, with, in, on, for*) unless they are the first word of a title.

   The Life **of** Thomas Edison   War **a**nd Peace   Death **of a** Salesman

Names of Organizations

1. Capitalize the names of organizations, government groups, and businesses.

   International **S**tudent **A**ssociation   the **S**enate   **G**estetner

2. Capitalize trade names, but do not capitalize the names of the product.

   IBM typewriter   **T**oyota hatchback   **K**ellogg's cereal

Other

1. Capitalize the names of languages

   Spanish   **T**hai   **F**rench   **J**apanese

2. Don't capitalize school subjects unless they are the names of languages or are followed by a number.

   geometry   **m**usic   **E**nglish   **A**rabic   **B**iology 306

APPENDIX **three**

Punctuation Rules

Period

1. Use a period after a statement or command.

   We are studying English.   Open your books to Chapter Three.

2. Use a period after most abbreviations.

   Mr.   Ms.   Dr.   Ave.   etc.   U.S.
   Exceptions: UN   NATO   IBM   AIDS

3. Use a period after initials.

H. G. Wells   Dr. H. R. Hammond

Question Mark

1. Use a question mark after (not before) questions.

Where are you going?   Is he here yet?

2. In a direct quotation, the question mark goes before the quotation marks.

He asked, "What's your name?"

Exclamation Point

Use an exclamation point after exclamatory sentences or phrases.

I won the lottery!   Be quiet!   Wow!

Comma

1. Use a comma before a conjunction (*and, or, so, but*) that separates two independent clauses.

She wanted to go to work, so she decided to take an English course.
He wasn't happy in that apartment, but he didn't have the money to move.

2. Don't use a comma before a conjunction that separates two phrases that aren't complete sentences.

She worked in the library and studied at night.
Do you want to go to a movie or stay home?

3. Use a comma before an introductory clause or phrase (generally if it is five or more words long).

After a beautiful wedding ceremony, they had a reception in her mother's home.
If you want to write well, you should practice writing almost every night.

4. Use a comma to separate interrupting expressions from the rest of a sentence.

Do you know, by the way, what time dinner is?
Many of the students, I found out, stayed on campus during the summer.

5. Use a comma after transitional expressions.

In addition, he stole all her jewelry.
However, he left the TV.

Common transitional expressions are:

therefore	in addition	in fact	on the other hand
consequently	moreover	similarly	for example
for this reason	furthermore	however	for instance
also	besides	nevertheless	

6. Use a comma to separate names of people in direct address from the rest of a sentence.

   Jane, have you seen Paul?
   We aren't sure, Mrs. Shapiro, where he is.

7. Use a comma after *yes* and *no* in answers.

   Yes, he was here a minute ago.
   No, I haven't.

8. Use a comma to separate items in a series.

   We have coffee, tea, and milk.
   He looked in the refrigerator, on the shelves, and in the cupboard.

9. Use a comma to separate an appositive from the rest of a sentence.

   Mrs. Sampson, his English teacher, gave him a good recommendation.
   Would you like to try a taco, a delicious Mexican food?

10. If a date or address has two or more parts, use a comma after each part.

    I was born on June 5, 1968.
    The house at 230 Seventh Street, Miami, Florida, is for sale.

11. Use a comma to separate contrasting information from the rest of the sentence.

    It wasn't Maria, but Parvin, who was absent.
    Bring your writing book, not your reading book.

12. Use a comma to separate quotations from the rest of a sentence.

    He asked, "What are we going to do?"
    "I'm working downtown," he said.

13. Use a comma to separate two or more adjectives that each modify the noun alone.

    She was an intelligent, beautiful actress. (*intelligent* and *beautiful* actress)
    Eat those delicious green beans. (*delicious* modifies *green beans*)

14. Use a comma to separate nonrestrictive clauses from the rest of a sentence. A nonrestrictive clause gives more information about the noun it describes, but it isn't needed to identify the noun. Clauses after proper names are nonrestrictive and require commas.

    It's a Wonderful Life, which is often on television at Christmastime, is my favorite movie.
    James Stewart, who plays a man thinking of killing himself, is the star of *It's a Wonderful Life*.

Quotation Marks

1. Use quotation marks at the beginning and end of exact quotations. Other punctuation marks go before the end quotation marks.

    He said, "I'm going to Montreal."
    "How are you?" he asked.

2. Use quotation marks before and after titles of stories, articles, songs, and television programs. Periods and commas go before the final quotation marks, while question marks and exclamation points normally go after them.

    Do you like to watch "Dallas" on television?
    My favorite song is "Let It Be."
    Do you like the story "Gift of the Magi"?

Apostrophes

1. Use apostrophes in contractions.

    don't   it's   we've   they're

2. Use an apostrophe to make possessive nouns.

    Singular: Jerry's   my boss's
    Plural: the children's   the Smiths'

Underlining

Underline the titles of books, magazines, newspapers, plays, and movies.

I am reading <u>One Hundred Years of Solitude.</u>
Did you like the movie <u>The Wizard of Oz</u>?

Student Name _____ Date _____

Personal reaction

_____

_____

_____

_____

Chapter Checklist	**Good**	**Needs Work**
1. Content		
a. Is the information about your partner interesting?	❏	❏
b. Is it complete?	❏	❏
c. Is it correct?	❏	❏
2. Organization		
a. Are all the sentences about one topic?	❏	❏
b. Is the order of the sentences easy to follow?	❏	❏
3. Cohesion and Style		
a. Are your sentences clear and simple?	❏	❏
b. Are they easy to understand?	❏	❏
c. Can you connect any sentences?	❏	❏
4. Grammar		
a. Is the grammar correct?	❏	❏
b. Are your verbs correct? Remember that third-person singular verbs end with *-s* in the present tense. Also check that your negative verbs are correct.	❏	❏
c. Are singular and plural nouns correct?	❏	❏
d. Is the word order in your sentences correct?	❏	❏
5. Form		
a. Is your punctuation correct?	❏	❏
b. Is your spelling correct?	❏	❏
c. Is your paragraph and sentence form correct?	❏	❏

Other comments

_____

_____

_____

_____

_____

CHAPTER two   *Feedback sheet*

Student Name _____   Date _____

Personal reaction

_____

_____

_____

_____

Chapter Checklist	<u>**Good**</u>	**Needs Work**
1. Content		
a. Are there interesting adjectives in the paragraph?	❏	❏
b. Do the adjectives describe the picture well?	❏	❏
2. Organization		
a. Does the paragraph move from general to specific?	❏	❏
b. Do you need to change the order of the sentences?	❏	❏
3. Cohesion and Style		
a. Can you connect any sentences?	❏	❏
b. Are the pronouns correct?	❏	❏
c. Are the adjectives in the correct place?	❏	❏
d. Are the prepositional phrases appropriate?	❏	❏
4. Grammar		
a. Are the verb forms correct? Is there an *-s* ending on all third-person singular verbs? (The use of the *-s* ending on verbs is subject-verb agreement.)	❏	❏
b. Is the use of *a/an* and *the* correct?	❏	❏
5. Form		
a. Does the paragraph follow the rules for correct form? If you aren't sure, look back at the rules for the form of a paragraph on pages 10 and 11, Chapter One.	❏	❏
b. Are the present participles correct?	❏	❏

Other comments

_____

_____

_____

_____

_____

Student Name _____ Date _____

Personal reaction

_____

_____

_____

_____

Chapter Checklist   <u>**Good**</u>   <u>**Needs Work**</u>

1. Content
   a. Is the paragraph interesting?   ❑   ❑
   b. Is the information clear?   ❑   ❑

2. Organization
   a. Does the topic sentence give the main idea of the paragraph?
       Is it a complete sentence?   ❑   ❑
   b. Are all the sentences about the holiday?   ❑   ❑
   c. Are the sentences in logical order?   ❑   ❑

3. Cohesion and Style
   a. Can you connect any sentences with *and, so,* or *but*? ❑   ❑
   b. Are the appositives correct?   ❑   ❑
   c. Does *such as* introduce examples?   ❑   ❑

4. Grammar
   a. Are the present-tense verbs correct?   ❑   ❑
   b. Are the count and noncount nouns correct?   ❑   ❑

5. Form
   a. Is the paragraph form (indentation, capitalization, and
       punctuation) correct?   ❑   ❑
   b. Is the spelling of words with *-s* endings correct? ❑   ❑
   c. Is the use of commas with appositives correct?   ❑   ❑

Other comments

_____

_____

_____

_____

_____

CHAPTER four

Student Name _____ Date _____

Personal reaction

_____

_____

_____

_____

Chapter Checklist

	Good	Needs Work
1. Content		
a. Are the activities interesting?	❏	❏
b. Are the directions clear?	❏	❏
2. Organization		
Is each paragraph about a different topic?	❏	❏
3. Cohesion and Style		
a. Are the propositions correct?	❏	❏
b. Is the use of *there* and *it* correct?	❏	❏
4. Grammar		
Are the verb forms correct?	❏	❏
5. Form		
a. Is the date correct?	❏	❏
b. Is the salutation correct?	❏	❏
c. Do the paragraphs begin with an indentation?	❏	❏
d. Is the closing in the right place?	❏	❏

Other comments

_____

_____

_____

_____

_____

_____

_____

_____

_____

Student Name _____ Date _____

Personal reaction

_____

_____

_____

_____

Chapter Checklist	**Good**	**Needs Work**
1. Content		
a. Is the information interesting?	❑	❑
b. Is the information important?	❑	❑
c. Is there an interesting title?	❑	❑
2. Organization		
a. Does the topic sentence give the main idea of the paragraph?	❑	❑
b. Are all the sentences about one topic?	❑	❑
c. Should you change the order of any of the sentences?	❑	❑
3. Cohesion and Style		
Did you combine sentences with time words and *and, but, so,* and *because*?	❑	❑
4. Grammar		
a. Are your nouns, pronouns, and articles correct?	❑	❑
b. Did you use good sentence structure (no sentence fragments)?	❑	❑
c. Did you use the correct past-tense verbs?	❑	❑
5. Form		
a. Did you use the correct paragraph form?	❑	❑
b. Did you capitalize the words in the title correctly?	❑	❑
c. Did you use correct punctuation when you combined sentences?	❑	❑

Other comments

_____

_____

_____

_____

_____

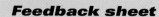

Student Name _____ Date _____

Personal reaction

_____

_____

_____

_____

Chapter Checklist	**Good**	**Needs Work**
1. Content		
a. Is the story clear?	❏	❏
b. Is all the information important?	❏	❏
2. Organization		
a. Did you use time words where necessary?	❏	❏
b. Did you add a title?	❏	❏
c. Should you change the order of any of the sentences?	❏	❏
3. Cohesion and Style		
a. Did you vary the time words and expressions?	❏	❏
b. Did you include enough description?	❏	❏
c. Did you use quotations?	❏	❏
4. Grammar		
a. Did you use the correct forms of the past tense?	❏	❏
b. Did you use the correct forms of the present continuous tense?	❏	❏
c. Did you use good sentence structure (no fragments)?	❏	❏
5. Form		
a. Did you use commas correctly?	❏	❏
b. Did you use quotation marks correctly?	❏	❏

Other comments

_____

_____

_____

_____

_____

_____

CHAPTER **seven** *Feedback sheet*

Student Name _____ Date _____

Personal reaction

_____

_____

_____

_____

Chapter Checklist	**Good**	**Needs Work**
1. Content		
a. Is the information interesting?	❏	❏
b. Are there purposes and examples in the paragraph?	❏	❏
2. Organization		
a. Does the topic sentence give the main idea of the paragraph?	❏	❏
b. Are all the sentences about the topic of the paragraph?	❏	❏
3. Cohesion and Style		
a. Did you use relative clauses correctly?	❏	❏
b. Did you use transitional words and phrases correctly?	❏	❏
c. Did you use quotations?	❏	❏
4. Grammar		
a. Did you use correct noun forms?	❏	❏
b. Did you use correct verb forms?	❏	❏
c. Did you use good sentence structure (no fragments)?	❏	❏
5. Form		
Are there commas after transitional words and after dependent clauses?	❏	❏

Other comments

_____

_____

_____

_____

_____

_____

_____

CHAPTER eight

Feedback sheet

Student Name _____ Date _____

Personal reaction

_____

_____

_____

_____

Chapter Checklist	Good	Needs Work
1. Content		
a. Is the title interesting?	❏	❏
b. Would other people want to see the movie because of your summary?	❏	❏
c. Did you present the problem and the events leading to the solution?	❏	❏
d. Does your summary include the type of movie, when and where the movie takes place, and the main character?	❏	❏
2. Organization		
a. Is all the information in the paragraph important?	❏	❏
b. Does the topic sentence give a general idea of what kind of movie you're writing about?	❏	❏
3. Cohesion and Style		
a. Did you combine sentences to show the relationship between events?	❏	❏
b. Did you use appositives correctly?	❏	❏
c. Did you use adjectives to describe the characters and the movie?	❏	❏
d. Did you use the historical present tense?	❏	❏
4. Grammar		
a. Are the present-tense verbs correct?	❏	❏
b. Are the count and noncount nouns correct?	❏	❏
c. Did you combine sentences correctly?	❏	❏
5. Form		
a. Did you underline the title of the movie?	❏	❏
b. Did you use commas with appositives and adjectives correctly?	❏	❏

Other comments

_____

_____

_____

CHAPTER nine   *Feedback sheet*

Student Name _____ Date _____

Personal reaction

_____

_____

_____

_____

Chapter Checklist	Good	Needs Work
1. Content		
a. Is the information interesting?	❏	❏
b. Is all the information in the paragraph important?	❏	❏
2. Organization		
a. Does the topic sentence give the main idea of the paragraph?	❏	❏
b. Are the sentences well organized?	❏	❏
c. Does the paragraph have a good concluding sentence?	❏	❏
3. Cohesion and Style		
a. Did you use transitional expressions correctly?	❏	❏
b. Did you use *so . . . that* correctly?	❏	❏
c. Did you use long forms rather than contractions as appropriate?	❏	❏
4. Grammar		
Did you use correct verb form?	❏	❏
5. Form		
a. Did you use commas correctly?	❏	❏
b. Did you spell the verb forms correctly?	❏	❏
c. Did you use correct capitalization?	❏	❏

Other comments

_____

_____

_____

_____

_____

_____

 **Feedback sheet**

Student Name _____ Date _____

Personal reaction

_____
_____
_____
_____

Chapter Checklist	**Good**	**Needs Work**
1. Content		
a. Is the information interesting?	❏	❏
b. Is there enough information?	❏	❏
2. Organization		
a. Did you list the holidays from most important to least important?	❏	❏
b. Did you give the same type of information about each holiday?	❏	❏
3. Cohesion and Style		
a. Did you use expressions such as *in addition to, besides, another, the first* (*second,* etc.)?	❏	❏
b. Did you use quantifiers correctly?	❏	❏
c. Did you use pronouns and pronominal expressions appropriately?	❏	❏
d. Did you use relative clauses correctly?	❏	❏
4. Grammar		
a. Are the verb forms correct?	❏	❏
b. Are there any sentence fragments?	❏	❏
5. Form		
Do the relative clauses have commas where necessary?	❏	❏

Other comments

_____
_____
_____
_____
_____
_____

Feedback sheet

Student Name _____ Date _____

Personal reaction

_____

_____

_____

_____

Chapter Checklist	**Good**	**Needs Work**
1. Content		
a. Does the message express your opinion strongly without personal attack?	❑	❑
b. Have you given reasons and examples to support your opinion?	❑	❑
2. Organization		
a. Are all your sentences on the topic on the newsgroup?	❑	❑
b. Does your message contain a sentence or two that gives the main idea of your message?	❑	❑
c. Does your topic line give the main idea of your message and make people want to read it?	❑	❑
3. Cohesion and Style		
a. Does your message use pronouns and synonyms to unify your writing?	❑	❑
b. Have you used polite phrases to give opinions and suggestions?	❑	❑
4. Grammar		
a. Are your verbs correct?	❑	❑
b. Have you used correct grammatical forms to give opinions and suggestions?	❑	❑
5. Form		
a. Have you avoided writing in all capitals?	❑	❑
b. Have you capitalized the important words in your topic line correctly?	❑	❑
c. Have you put brackets in front of lines quoting other messages?	❑	❑
d. Have you written a signature under your message with your name and electronic address?	❑	❑

Other comments

_____

_____

_____

CHAPTER twelve — *Feedback sheet*

Student Name _____ Date _____

Personal reaction

_____

_____

_____

_____

Chapter Checklist	**Good**	**Needs Work**
1. Content Did you explain the problem clearly?	❏	❏
2. Organization **a.** Did you include all the necessary details?	❏	❏
b. Did you include any unnecessary details?	❏	❏
3. Cohesion and Style **a.** Did you use formal language?	❏	❏
b. Did you use polite language?	❏	❏
4. Grammar **a.** Did you use correct verb forms?	❏	❏
b. Did you use past participles as adjectives correctly?	❏	❏
5. Form Did you use the correct business letter format, with a date, inside address, salutation, and closing?	❏	❏

Other comments

_____

_____

_____

_____

_____

_____

_____

_____

_____